The Heart as Framed
New & Select Poems

THE HEART AS FRAMED

New and Select Poems

Richard Jackson

Press 53

Winston-Salem

Press 53, LLC
PO Box 30314
Winston-Salem, NC 27130

First Edition

Silver Concho Poetry Series
edited by Pamela Uschuk and William Pitt Root

Library of Congress Control Number
2022933690

Printed on acid-free paper
ISBN 978-1-950413-48-5

For Terri

Also by Richard Jackson

Poems
Part of the Story
Worlds Apart
Alive All Day
Svetovi Narazen (Slovenia)
Heart's Bridge (Limited Edition)
Heartwall
Half Lives
Unauthorized Autobiography
Resonance
Retrievals
Resonancia (Barcelona)
Out of Place
Traversings (with Robert Vivian)
Broken Horizons
Where The Wind Comes From

Translations
Last Poems: Selected Poems of Pascoli
(Italian, with Susan Thomas, Deborah Brown)
Potovanje Sonca (*Journey of the Sun*) by Alexsander Persola
(Slovene)

Chapbooks
Falling Stars
Fifties
Cesare Pavese: The Woman in the Land (translation)
Greatest Hits 1980-2004
Strays

Criticism
The Dismantling of Time in Contemporary American Poetry
Acts of Mind: Interviews with Contemporary Poets

Edited Anthologies
The Fire Under The Moon: Contemporary Slovene Poetry
Double Vision: Four Slovenian Poets (with Aleš Debeljak)
A Bridge of Voices (online e-book, with Barbara Carlson)

The Heart's Many Doors: American Poets Respond to Metka Krašovec's
Images Responding to Emily Dickinson

Edited Books
Tomaž Salamun, Ko vdre senca/When the Shadow Breaks
Iztok Osojnik: Selected Poems
Iztok Osojnik, Wagner (co-editing with others)

ACKNOWLEDGMENTS

Ecstasy (Anthology), "The Fire in the Soul: A World Without Angels"

Georgia Review, "In the Time of the Living"

Cutthroat: A Journal of the Arts, "Columbine," "A World Without Angels"

James Dickey Review, "The Tides," "Quantum Entanglement," "The Truth of It"

Asheville Poetry Review, "Thermal Time," "The Rivers (rev)," "Elegy Just in Case," "Elegey for the Late Conjunctions of the Fall"

Brilliant Corners, "Listening to Coltrane's Alabama," "13th and Elm," "Not the Same Moon," "Elaine, Arkansas 1919," "Elegy with No Real Ending," "Night Vision: Kind of Blue," "Whole Notes, Feb. 20, 1980"

One, "Theory of Touch"

B O D Y, "Rione Sant'Angelo," "A Train: The Scotsboro Boys"

Truth To Power (anthology), "The Barbed Wire"

North American Review, "Elegy Walking Through the Woods," "Hosea's Appeal" River River, "Invisibility"

Thanks to the following Presses for first publishing some of these poems in other books: Grove Press (*Part of the Story*); University of Alabama Press (*Worlds Apart*); Cleveland State University Press (*Alive All Day*); University of Massachusetts Press (*Heartwall*); C&R Press (*Retrievals*); Autumn House (*Half Lives*); Ashland Poetry Press (*Unauthorized Autobiography*; *Resonance*; *Out of Place*); Anchor and Plume Press (*Traversings*); Press 53 (*Broken Horizons*); Kelsay Press (*Where the Wind Comes From*)

No language but the language of the heart
                                    —Alexander Pope

With better knowledge how the heart was framed....
                              —Wordsworth, *1799 Prelude*

I carry inside my heart
As in a chest too full to shut
All the places where I've been.
                              —Pessoa

...whereabouts unknown inside my heart
                                    —Rumi

My heart makes songs on lonely roads.
                                    —Ivor Gurney

          The two
heart-grey puddles:
two
mouthsfull of silence.
                    —Paul Celan

In the last chamber of the heart
all the words are hanging
but one
          —WS Merwin

Do not let your hearts be troubled and do not be afraid.
                                    —John 14:27

CONTENTS

NEW POEMS

WHERE THE WIND COMES FROM (2021)

BROKEN HORIZONS (2018)

TRAVERSINGS (2016)

OUT OF PLACE (2014)

RETRIEVALS (2013)

RESONANCE (2010)

HALF LIVES: PETRARCHIAN POEMS (2004)

UNAUTHORIZED BIOGRAPHY (2003)

HEARTWALL (2000)

ALIVE ALL DAY (1992)

WORLDS APART (1987)

PART OF THE STORY (1983)

NEW POEMS

Rione Sant'Angelo,
Outside La Taverna Del Ghetto

Halos of mist wrap around the streetlights.
Every sound is pocketed. Birds who think
they are angels wonder why there are no answers
for what they sing. Dusk begins to sift
through the mist. The woman carrying her life,
who passed by a moment ago, calls out
from the next street and someone answers,
but not to her. There are no angels here.
The halos quiver. A single bird drinks
from a street puddle. The sky leans down
onto the shoulders of buildings. She calls out
again. She thinks she has been here before.
Time starts to wobble on its axis. The robin
can't find its nest. There are sounds
with no source, roots that lose their way
and break the sidewalk's surface. There is
the news from my own borders. There is
a stone wall that stretches fifty feet
but marks nothing, belongs to nothing,
stands for nothing. Only the cats still play
on broken pillars and arches, as they did
during the roundup of October, 1943.
Today's newspaper has a smudged date.
In the distance a shaft of light falls on
nothing in particular. Again the call.
There is nothing to say, nothing to do,
nowhere to go. My own watch stutters its alarm.

Listening to Coltrane's "Alabama"
as the Perseids Fade Out

Nothing can explain how to love a world
that sets the heart's clock always out of synch,
where the meanings of our words are ambushed
by the kind of hate that becomes the 16th Street
Baptist Church bombing, Sept 15, 1963,
nothing to explain the way Coltrane's horn
starts to speak over a trembling bass, tracing
over the words of King's eulogy, borrowing
phrases and cadences until the pressure mounts
into a collision of dirges as if the music itself
were trying to speak.
                        Nothing to explain how
when I first read the story in the *Eagle-Tribune*
I still believed our dreams meant something that
we would find out later. Even now the day begins
to leech into the night the way a few hopeful
notes seems to hover like doves over the band,
or the way Anaximander described the world
as a silent rock floating in space.
                        Now it seems
Coltrane's whole quartet has entered the church,
everyone going everywhere to arrive at the same
note. I can see a thin line of grief shimmer on
the ridgeline. Four girls, Addie, Denise, Carole,
Cynthia, one of them beheaded beneath the rubble.
I can't imagine. I cannot imagine. All I can know
is the way Coltrane lets me into my own soul
for it is the music that brings us all together.

The wind tried for hours to rearrange the dust.
One story followed another like geese until there was
no story, no trial, no conviction. When Coltrane
came in over McCoy Tyner's piano and its slow lament
he already knew the future was exactly the past.
The silences and pauses tell a story these words cannot.

Coltrane didn't play music, he played the heart. Here,
even the insects seem to have stopped out of respect.
There's a wind that is not even a wind in the trees.

Anaximander knew our world was a box whose
sides were endless. Coltrane knew our world was
the church whose sides collapsed. *Alabama*—
all he needed was that one word, rolling down
the register and trying to lift itself at the end with
a desperate sigh.
                   I am writing this just north of
the state of Alabama, the meteors in the darkened sky
telling the same stories Anaximander heard, or maybe
the dreams of four girls still wandering off ahead of them
forever. Now Coltrane, too, seems to cry at the end, and
if you listen close you'll swear you hear his voice
whispering against the stories that set the killers free,
stories that staggered along the courthouse halls
until too late.
                   The music stops and you have to play it
again just to try to breathe. The first shadows on the lake
start to blot out the stars. There's nothing to tell the owl
who continues to accuse us all, nothing to tell even
the fish who continue to nibble at the surface of the water
as if to test, then reject the only world they can see.

The Perseids go on silently year after year, and tonight
there's nothing to explain how the soul's music laments
its own music, a music now lost in the pure music of grief.

Elegy Walking Through the Woods

an angel comes to me and taps
my lips
                    —Ralph Angel

There's a touch, as if of a passing cloud, that we hardly
feel until later. It's the chill that time leaves behind,
the track that tells you who or what has passed before,
the grass folded down where the deer spent the night.

That morning, for instance, when my dog lay two weeks
on the spot where her companion died. She knew
not death but an absence that filled her heart
with the darkness of migrant stars.
                                        You can walk away
from a place but not its time.
                                Or else, the footbridge
here I can no longer cross after another loss.
                                                I am
walking on an ancient riverbed high above the river
that tells us how we are poured out like water.
There are millennia stored in the earth beneath me.
There are times, standing still, when you can feel
the earth move again revealing our loneliness
among the depth of years.
                            How cold now,
the late day's light. There are innumerable prayers
nesting in the trees. A coyote flickers between
the trunks. The fish lie dormant in their dreams
among the boulders strewn about, —what you would
have called gifts from the cliffs above them.
                                            Now daylight
starts to find a place to hide among the caves and hollows.
An owl has left behind what it hunted as a sign
we are never safe.
                    Some of these words have hunted for
an easy consolation,

> yet how deftly the wind whispers
your angel's voice through the spare winter branches,
how fragile this horizon of birds whose name I have lost.

There's a strange evening light that seems to linger
in the woods beneath the darkness, what my father
called *tomorrow's spirits.*
> It seems right, now, to walk
among them, while the sun sets, while a full moon
begins to rise among the spare lines of a few cirrus clouds.

I've opened that moonlight knowing you are there.

—*Little River Canyon, AL*

In The Time of The Living

I who have always believed too much in words.
                    —Remembering WS Merwin

How often we imagine the sounds of buried insects.
How often our words are the ghosts of those we've lost.
So many moments are filled with their own endings.
By the time we think we hear it the airliner is
already out of sight. Our lives dissipate like its
ice crystal vapor trails against the early moonlight
from winds too high to hear. Each night the deafening
sounds of stars die before they reach us. Their light
bends so much they are never where we see them.
High over the gorge this afternoon an eagle whistled
a cry we could almost hear. These are cries, you said,
frozen in another age. How often we believe in nothing
as if it is something we trust, like a blind man tracing
the circle he will walk. He doesn't see the heron who
disguises itself as a spring sapling while watching
the fish watch him. An otter and its shadow disappear
down the muddy riverbank. Meanwhile, news of
your passing glides in along gravitational waves
we can't feel from places we can't see. The heron
hasn't moved. There are distant highway sounds
and the sounds of the attacks on trees, on water, on air.
There are the silenced voices of the latest massacre.
Whole galaxies collect themselves in eddies and currents
that will someday wash over us. How easy it is to back
into these darkest of worlds. The heron lurches off
following the river's meander downstream as if he were
a divining rod. Once, far from here, the Northern Lights
seemed to glide over me on their enormous wings.
I am trying to believe in a world whose name I can't
pronounce. In this way we become metaphors for how
we want to live, even as our own dreams take flight.
We say two planets line up with the moon, but that is only
what we see from here. They care nothing at all for our
geometry or beliefs. Zecharius' visions of horses as wind and
trees as countries tell us there is a hidden world living inside

this one. It is like the world the heron knows beneath the water.
Words we say are doors that led to dark or light passages.
Maybe we will all be born into another language whose
words hover like those new dragonflies refusing to land
before they die. That is why we never want the poems to end.
That is why the heron traces his own shadow up and down
the river. The rowers have no idea of the drama he has been
writing, of these words rippling the surface before they vanish.
A bat's silent sounding shudders against the coming wall of night.
The heron drops whatever past he's been holding in his bill.

Sidestepping Love Poem

For Terri

It was when the robins congregated in the trees
that I dreamt they were singing for you.
                                        It was
winter and a single rose still swayed in the wind
saying something about sidestepping time.
                                        I could
barely hear. Later, I watched a few reluctant stars
argue about what constellations they would join
in the next millennia.
                        Where are we if the dream
in which we find ourselves has no exit?
                                        My words are

turning into clouds.
                        I've read how species of trees
connect through mycelium threads beneath
the ground.
                Maybe that is what the robins were
singing.
                Something of love goes on when we're gone.

It is like the stromatolites, the oldest living fossils
on earth, flat stony stepping stones still colonized
by layers of tiny organisms.
                                Just crumpling up
the calendar page doesn't crumple up the past.

I know, these metaphors grow like those fossils.

But here we are on a day like any other except
for its number, hearing the robins sing, listening
to stars and talking to trees, stepping over or
sidestepping time, because what more can love do?

Two Worlds

I thought it was Pauli who said two objects couldn't occupy
the same space at the same time, but he was talking about
electrons, and I didn't know any of that until much later
and besides, from the ground floor I was already
transported by the corn beef and cabbage my Irish Aunt was
cooking on the third floor
                              where I could see myself lying
on her Sears rug under the eye of her Philco radio, my
eyes following how the wheels on the toy fire engine
kept turning in place as the engine moved on its way
into some imagined world that appeared in the next
sweep across the floor
                         and because there are so many
worlds stacked over this one, I can't explain why
it would be years before that memory sifted down through
the decades, as if through the fog embracing Sansepolcro
on my way to Pierro's "Resurrection" and Christ's eyes
stalking me around the hall with their *trompe- l'oeil*
sight lines, and it seemed He was about to step from
the painting, one foot in the tomb, the other resting on its lip,
as if to occupy life and death, heaven and hell at once,

just as I was, standing before the Roman tomb and two
misplaced Corinthian columns, but also standing with Pierro
as he dreams through the Spring and Autumn on either side
of Christ, and as the soldier in brown armor, his self-portrait,
(according to Vasari) trying to sleep unaware below Christ,
and I remembered that this was where Aldous Huxley stood
occupying this same space who thought our own world might be
another world's hell, and who loved this painting best of all,
or at least as much as the artillery officer, Tony Clarke,
who refused to fire on Pierro's art as the Nazis left, standing
here, on this site of another battle painted by Leonardo,
horses and riders merging into each other's space though
the painting is lost behind Vasari's own fresco in Firenze,

occupying its own unseen world except for a few sketches
and copies,
             but it is those eyes, still following me, and
foreseeing all this, but maybe trying to say how we are
all connected by invisible lines of sight, that brings me back
to my aunt's store-bought copies of thatched cottages and Nativities,
sacred scenes greener than Piero's, that hung on her walls as if
to transport her to some space before the peat farmers, before
the British occupiers of County Mayo, before *the troubles*,
before the potato famine, before all the protests and
riots that once streamed below her balcony above
Hall street over the signs, *Irish Need Not Apply*, because,
as Piero knew, we can live inside a painting despite
the physics, despite the clocks, pausing as Christ paused
to include everything we see within the frame and
everything we don't see outside it, including us
rising up out of it into a world we must make anew.

A Train: The Scottsboro Boys

There is no such thing as past or future.
                    —Carlo Rovelli

There is nothing to stop you, hearing the box cars
clanging into one another in the Chattanooga freight
yard, beyond where the moon presses like a fist
into the ridgeline, nothing to stop you from imagining
them hopping the freight safely all the way to Memphis
despite knowing how inside each box car is a place
we never finally reach.

                    Not History then but their last free
night simply one of heavy rain pressing against the supple
fields further on down the line, that is, Painted Rock,
a stop that shouldn't be a stop except for

                                        the story
the two white women will not retract, despite the fact
that inside each story we tell another writes itself,

but there is nothing now to stop you from imagining
that maybe they do not throw the white kids off the train,
leaving no witnesses, that the sheriff does not hold them,

that instead he stands amazed at how the crows
witness this from the broken branches of a dead tree,
or the grass seems to flow in unconcerned rivulets,

and you do not have to see the boys themselves shackled
and wondering what it was back before Chattanooga,
before Scottsboro,

                    where children's kites seem to them to be
pointing, no, jabbing accusations, though they too are
hidden over the hill,

                    but maybe it is just the first birds
collecting their own stories to build another nest, the fox's
blur against the trees.

No, it is the way, like Coleridge,
we can see or say, but not feel, what they felt, and find
ourselves hopeless as the landscape, distant as those crows
that can't understand.

And months from now, maybe years,
still enough time for another version where each tree does
not hold a future club, each vine not a rope, that inside
each death is not another death,
for this is your story to make
and it will not disappear the way our shadows do when
we die as the child once asked,
a child not much older than
the gator bait children of the twenties, or the Wrightsville
School boys of 1959, their stories padlocked in a room
the size of a box car and burned,

all of which appear here
because inside each word some memory stalks another
memory and without hearing it you know it is there,
because however little we understand today as we are,
our words embrace all of us, however distant,
the way our dreams continue on without us,
the way one star spills its light against another star
beyond what we will ever see, where time echoes
back and forth in their light

and there is nothing here
to stop you from imagining a way to uncouple the story,
and even if we were to return you would not even know
where you were, the clouds covered with footsteps, the tracks
failing, the dreamt landscape yielding to that distant day,

March 25, 1931, waxing moon, calm wind, a steel chill,
the beginning broken, the end beginning, trying to love
what is human and failing, despite what seems to travel
now in the boxcars of the heart, one hate inside another hate.

13TH and Elm

If you are reading this you know how *The White Elephant Saloon*
was brought down by the big game hunters we call Foundries,
near Blue Goose Hollow, home of Bessie Smith, home of
the foundlings, the forgotten, the dispossessed, a flood zone,
as it turned out, though it never stopped the music. If you
go now you'll find 13th and Elm no longer exists, for even now
the wind and river seem to whisper the laments no one wants
to hear, no one wants to remember. She could feel the stares
that seem to scope them as they always did from beyond the
hollow. Even now her soul sings a language everyone knows.
"Laughing to keep from Crying" is how Langston Hughes
put it. But there are scars that never get resolved. She
and her brother performed there, ten years old, marveling
at the notes that came from their own emptiness. What passed
for sewers overran. What passed for darkness grew darker.
Even today the darkness has not quite vanished from there.
Even today the young horns and guitars echo through the streets.
They do not forget how she escaped the chains of the producers,
they do not forget, not the stops and searches, not the refusals,
not the invisible neighborhoods, not what Phillip Williams calls
their "inheritance," that is, how the "spring noose clears its throat."
If you are reading this you know how it ends but we can't end
there. There were always the mountains, and beyond them,
dreams neither she nor we have words for except the names
of cities that meant only the music of their sounds. If you go,
you have to go not knowing if you will return, or even if you will
arrive. The lights there extend the day like whole notes, like
the way she draws out each measure that turns the darkness blue.
Love seemed to check in and out on schedule the way each
verse opened up a story that wasn't a story she didn't live.
I don't think the record producers who cheated her understood that.
The year she died Rogers and Hart wrote *My Funny Valentine*,
1937. *You make me smile with my heart*, it goes, though it was
Chet Baker's 1952 horn that seemed to be crying to keep
from laughing, as Langston might have added. Sometimes

our words tell a truth of their own. Across the river the cliffs
keep the same silence they always have. The shadows of trees
seem to dance when the wind picks up. The geese on the river, too,
catch it on their way, like us, to wherever it takes them. Sunset
seems to burn the ridge line. The broken factories turn the other
sky gray. What do we know except a song has changed a life?
I think we have to measure things by those words and notes.
I think we have to measure things by where we are not.
If you are reading this you know what I am trying to say, what
these ghosts, their music, have hid behind their words. *When you get
good lovin', never go and spread the news,* Bessie sang, though
she did, night after night, and if you are reading this, if you go
there, you know what I mean, smiling with your heart, night after night.

Facing East

For Terri

There are fragments of sky stored in the coyotes' calls.
All night they answer the ambulances with a mournful prayer.
It is said the Lakota followed the Wolf to learn how to hunt.
Tonight the woods smell of Spring and memory.
One night four coyote pups dug a future in the garden beneath
our window. Their whimper seemed half ecstasy, half lament
for having escaped their den. They had not yet learned
about the owl's shadow tracing its own meanings in the earth.
Lately there have been too many deaths. Even our own words
seem masked. What we say is heard and disappears like
the flash of a firefly. The daffodils, too, have come and gone.
There, another siren, but also another prayer. The mockingbird
wants to become all of us. The leaves are turning into compost.
This afternoon we watched the Gypsy Moth larvae crawl
from eggs and begin to explore the web's surface. Their call
must be at a pitch we cannot hear. You've placed the new hive
facing east so the bees can warm themselves and begin the job
of collecting the first sunlight. Inside, their murmur brings
home wherever they have been. I think it is our prayer
for whatever flowers. This is the way we hold the sky
in our hearts. We are living on the edge of whatever sings.

Elegy for the Late Conjunctions of the Fall

It's life that suddenly fills both ears with the sound of a symphony
that forces your pulse to race and swells your heart near to bursting.
                                                —Marvin Bell

While the breeze, on high, sang a lullaby, the tune goes.
A lullaby that goes the way Chet Baker's wistful trumpet
played Cole Porter's lyrics
                        while the stars you saw and
the stars you didn't see are connected now by the vapor
trail of some plane that points, not home, but someplace
we have never been.
                        Now it is already approaching Winter.
The early frost begins to score constellations of notes
on the windows and fallen leaves.
                        A few urban coyotes
try to compete with the scream of an ambulance.

A neighbor's dog is fooled into answering just off key.

We hardly ever hear what we hear, hardly ever see
what we see. You could hear the blind stars sing too,
but what was that?
                Under stars chilled by the winter,
Chet Baker played on, played, like you, by ear, because
that, you said, was all we had,
                        counting your own rhythm
with your finger while you read.
                        Tonight, like two stars
above the ridge's dark brow, on this night of a waxing
moon, Jupiter and Saturn start to approach each other
before separating,
                music of the spheres they once called it.

Tonight the solar wind we never see or hear, trumpets
stellar dust across the galaxies, arriving as usual from
constellations that exploded billions of years ago.

The world is remade from these endings.

                                        Tonight, a barred
owl,
     hearing the stars sing, the planets dance, the coyotes
answer, even, I swear, hearing Chet Baker's trumpet scatter
its own stellar dust as I listen now, as the whole universe listens,
as you did that last morning,
                               has delayed the end of its song.

Elaine, Arkansas, 1919

. . .cutting off the ears or toes of dead negroes
for souvenirs and the dragging of their bodies
through the streets of Elaine, . . .other bodies thrown
into a pit and burned or hanging from a bridge
outside of Helena.
                        —NYT, Sept 20, 2019

Not the elegy, no, but the poem about the elegy,
the curtain, the way light refracts the path of trout,
or air deflects the position of stars.

                                    It's the emptiness
of words themselves, meanings changing shape
with the clouds.

                        These hairline fractures of the heart,
these chokeholds on our dreams.

                                    A whole town
of amnesiacs. The streetlights arched towards
the road like the bodies they once held. The ditch
still smoldering its invisible history.

                                    I remember
as a boy wondering why the deer was so riddled
senselessly with bullets, but that is nothing
when compared to what happens to the bodies
left charred or gutted.

                        There is an emptiness
so huge we can't tell if we are in it, or it in us.

"Sad but True" sang Gwendolyn Elaine
Armstrong on her only cut (King Records).
Named for the town and Satchmo, among
the first to break barriers at the University
of Mississippi, she sang words into notes,—
so not an elegy, then, but a love song,

                                    When
you listen you feel how, even now, each
hour counterpoints another to escape

the night of all those souls inhabiting
this storm of fireflies, bats lost in their own
echoes, circling the cicadas that witness
what we must not forget.
                              Not an elegy then,
but a lament for the soul's prisoners.
                              A break
in the melody where an accusing history rushes in.

Elegy Along a Line of Sight

. . .the good times kept singing, kept rolling, until
his heart stopped, called him to hurry home.
                    —Jon Tribble, "Is You Is or Is You Ain't"

The deer grazing under the eye of the wolf moon
pay no attention to the way it hunts, nor to
the Red Tail Hawk knifing its way towards
a vole, or maybe to a rabbit just out of sight among
the tall grasses, now, just before dusk turns
to night.
                Tourists lining the battlefield road
take a few photos by the monuments.
They think they can hold back a time that's already
marching in shadows across the meadow.

They don't notice how the far jagged ridge is
outlined by a quivering line of light from
the approaching storm.
                        It was here the 1st
Arkansas Volunteers marched towards a future
that is already smoke.
                    You can almost see
the wind hold its breath, waiting.
                            In another
Century, maybe—no. you would not.
                            It is not
important to know where our truths come from,
only that they arrive.
                    Back in town, everything is
in a hurry—distant sirens, horns, the moan of semis
along GA route 2, the plane's engine powering down,
returning from its stopover.
                        But that hawk. There is
my own story I never finished about the feathers of
the Red Tail mixed with some nameless fur I found
one morning.
                It, too, is a story neither of us finished.
Ground fog, as thick as musket smoke from the lost
battles here, starts to embrace the deer.

                              The growl
of the storm, too, means something it wants to say.

The lives here sputtered like the night fires each unit
kept against the sudden freeze.
                              The heart's rain
falls like bees spilling from a hive, you wrote.

How seldom we can see our way to say what we love.

The eye of the storm always seems to close before we finish.

.

Invisibility

Here the invisible is what one cannot cease to see.
—Maurice Blanchot

It was the mysterious call from something hidden
beyond the swamp.
                    Or it was the glow from a distant
fire or service station out on the highway, and not
the sunset I hoped for.
                    And there was the deer hardly
touching earth, disappearing, as the coyote chased it
towards where the stones marking where the old battle lines
march into and out of memory.
                    Here even the past
tries to be visible.
                    Further back a few restless ghosts
that seem to follow like the clouds of gnats, or inhabit
the sound of the unseen grouse.
                    Further back the ancient
microbes and viruses hidden in the icepack, uncovered
in fossils and shadowy species.
                    In the end, isn't the invisible
what we most want to see, just as much as we fear it?

You might remember Katherine Johnson, one of NASA's
hidden figures, feared for her color so that she herself
kept nearly invisible, whose invisible numbers created
a visible world that arranged pathways through the stars.

Above us, Johnson's moon reveals an ancient world
of asteroids beneath its surface.
                    Here the silence is all
we see: tracks hardened in the mud, trenches become
long depressions those soldiers took refuge in.
                    Clouds
seem to palm the surface of the tall grass. That deer
has long disappeared though it continues, invisible,
in these lines.

Above, the stars are still hidden but Venus
announces itself with the borrowed light of the sunset.
The stars hold back their light like dreamers. Here's what
Johnson knew: that all our numbers only mark a relation
to other numbers without which we all amount to zero,
that we only mean to others what we mean to ourselves,
that the love we take is equal to the love we give as the song
said, "I can see you without my eyes," Rilke prayed to God,
that it is too easy to become as invisible as the stick
figures erased on a child's magic slate or screen.

Whole Notes Feb 20, 1980

If a man wishes to be sure of the road he treads on,
he must close his eyes and walk in the dark.
                —John of the Cross, *The Dark Night of the Soul*

        Then you set my very soul on fire.
                —"Carless Love Blues"

From where the Union Soldiers messaged their plans,
1863, from Signal Mountain where I traced stars
flickering like pinging light bulbs about to go dark
from where Chattanooga was just a glow from
the town below,
                the news came. The five women
emerging from the *Whole Note*. Ninth Street, now
MLK street. Shot.

                Their evening had walked for days over
the cinders of the abandoned trolley bed just to be there.
Such news back then arrived like a fox stealing
its way along the tree line, or embers whispering to reveal
the truths we can't ignore.
                        I imagined them hearing
some version of Betsy Smith's "Careless Love Blues,"
echoing from where she grew up a few blocks away,
imagined their emotions sliding along the register from
excitement to torture to anger as Betsy did in 1925.

I imagined it was the song itself that saved them.

But that is part of the faulty scaffolding of our hearts,
a tangle of dreams collapsing and rebuilding so that
something is always missing or added unsuspectingly
like the extra beat my heart tacks on now and then.

In fact, my new neighbor said, during the riots and
protests "Don't worry. We have our Blacks under control."

"You nearly spoiled this life of mine / That's why I sing
this song of hate," Betsy lamented and what I thought,
imagining the five women must have too. "All my
happiness bereft."

All night, the loose talk of insects made
no more sense than the voices surrounding me. I knew
my flashlight told me only how close the night had stalked
us. I knew the four Klansmen would not sing her words
"For my sins, 'til judgment I'll atone."

I knew from Hayden's
poem how Bessie "shone that smile on us and sang" because
she knew her voice outlived them all.

I knew to leave
the mountain. I knew how to choose between the life lived
and the life imagined. I wondered what stars will appear
long after we have gone, and if we will ever learn
the words we have to learn if we are ever to escape
the smoke-filled soul, the catacombs of the heart.

Night Vision, Kind of Blue

River Pretty, 2019

Tonight as we hear the hidden rivers that flow inside
the river, can almost hear the invisible maps of geese,
listen to the highways of the air the bee follows, see
the trout's hidden compass braving the currents we know
just by a ripple of water,
                        a canoe had caught itself on
the shallow rapids, its occupants frantically pushing off
the rocks, the past and future just a set of possibilities
so that now you are probably asking what all this means
and how many worlds exist beside the one we see.

"Don't play what's there, play what's not there,"
Miles Davis famously said. And we do.
                             Here,
in the bar on river we've turned to "Blue in Green,"
one mood, one vision inside another.
                           But those
canoeists, searching for a single melody to carry
them downstream—science tells us that all
we know are interactions, not things—one world,
one word, inside another.
                    It's the way
Bill Evans' piano current delicately opens and then
glides beneath Miles' searching trumpet.
                         There is
so much we don't hear, so much we don't see.

A few whitecaps show where hidden rocks wait.
A great blue heron traces the route the canoeists
should have taken.
                  Evans' piano fades to nothing
or maybe emerges as if he wanted to start again, like
the curved space that takes us back to the beginning,
like the river east of here that reversed direction,
like stars somewhere still ablaze as dawn unfolds.

Thermal Time

Time is information we don't have. Time is our ignorance.
—Carlo Rovelli

You could have read about blankets of sound
from nesting doves in sonorous pentameters,
or the milkweed nodding in the early breeze
of some pastoral love poem where bales of
golden hay line up for review in the pasture, or
read Ptolemy's visions guided by the daily phases
of the pale halfmoon looking carefully over it all,—

did you think that would be enough to let you
forget the two Palestinian boys shot in Gaza?

Then turn instead to a few stanzas below us
where the burnt-out hulks of a car have melted
into a Police Station wall in Nairobi. If you
don't like that, turn the page to where thorns
of light have begun to pierce through the branches,
where the tracks of history are still fresh,
where the camp survivor lists the names of
the corpses she was made to shovel into ditches.
What she is saying is that time is reversable,
not to change, but to live again in our ignorance.

Now the evening wind begins to breathe its last.
The child next door trembles when the man comes home.
For the mother there is no past. Every clock tells its own lie.
The soul stands mute. It is so much easier to read
about orchards and oceans, whatever shape we give
to the world the way the Greeks named constellations
to allay their fear of what lay beyond.

                        Do you think
all this has an end or a beginning? Tell me, where
does a wave begin? A mountain? The decision
to pull the trigger? Words for that dissolve into air
quicker than we can say them. But go ahead, whatever

doubts you had will follow you through these woods
like clouds of gnats. Above you, acres of burnt
branches web the air. *Who did all this?* some politician
asked Picasso of his *Guernica. You did,* he answered.

You don't like the picture *you* are facing? Have you
figured out why the rabbit never expects the hawk?
By now the doves have moved on to begin another day
that has already forgotten us. The flame returns its atoms
to begin it all again. The moon grows paler only
to become pure sky.

                    Somewhere, before any of this,
a young child crawls out of the ruins from a drone strike
or a mortar round, maybe a vest bomb, and she too will
face a choice, for the light seems to blister the air
around her, but this is also yours to write, perhaps
to bless, or even love, for it is a message you'll have
to write if you want to live among the creatures of
the earth, knowing how the moon is slowly drifting away,
the cosmos receding, the time beginning to melt away from us.

Autumnal

*When you arise in the morning, think of what
a precious privilege it is to be alive - to breathe,
to think, to enjoy, to love.*
                    —Marcus Aurelius

for Barbara Hurd and Stephen Dunn

Despite the fact that even this early the night tries
to leave traces of itself beneath the cliffs and trees,
that a small plane seems to be chasing after the last stars
whose fading light, the legend goes, mark the last
flickers of countless loves, despite the fact that
the fading ivy vine writes its desperate story up
the sides of the dying oak, or that a few fireflies
seem confused in the shadows of the pine stand,
there are your words by which a fearful future
keeps its distance, by which the creek whispers
itself into another age, the mourning doves search
a new way to call to each other, for every love is
a secret as secure as the meanings of petroglyphs,
for everywhere now the gaps in the swaying trees
keep recalculating our geometries, and it is not
the clouds but the hills that seem to move, as now
we have learned of a new comet that follows
no one's trail, hidden as the far river's course is
by white brushstrokes of fog, while here the spider
beneath the porch begins to reconsider the broken
web's location as if it could follow any of its
radiating strands, like the bees storing up their
futures, the roots grappling deeper for winter,
like anyone who would understand the light within
the light this morning, who knows that even
the faintest animal trail, like the smallest vein, will
lead always back to our hearts, to ourselves, to the stars,
the trees, the breaths, the rivers that keep going on.

Not the Same Moon

"The moon is the same moon above you,"
Ella Fitzgerald still sings on the scratched
1961 vinyl, but it isn't. There is a noose
hanging from a Live Oak just south of here
like an empty moon, like a half note,
like the frayed circle the swifts make spiraling
around the abandoned factory stack. Tonight,
listening to her, every note comes around
changed and hiding its unspoken word, for
"A Night in Tunisia" is what she sang, but
behind it "Interlude" lurked, where Sarah Vaughan
sang "Love's a passing interlude," and it is.

Tonight the sirens are answering a 911 call,
shots fired, *enroute*, the web page says, and later,
victim's name withheld. Then on to the next call.
Where it heads is just a question of geography.
Tonight, the clouds again claim no name, the birds
that used to arrive no longer arrive, and what birds
remain take their songs with them, while everywhere
the music of emptiness grows ever more empty.

Sometimes I think Ella's moon changes faces
to warn us. Someone says the moon is off its leash.
Someone else says the moon has its own song.
I can almost hear the hush of its shadows.
I can almost hear the night flowers opening to its light.

The shimmering notes of crickets announces their own
tentative music. The cicadas hesitate, for they must
wait for the exact temperature, then screech for their mates.
"The ending of day brings release" Ella continues.
It is not the same moon, no, but we listen anyway, for
our minds are windmills testing the compass points.

The Tides

There was no one sleeping// who did not dream of being touched. . .
     —Tony Hoagland, "In a Quiet Town by the Sea"

Another shimmering fog shrouds the harbor lighthouse
signaling a freighter's running lights
that blemish the horizon.
Just offshore a rusted skiff's an amulet riding the heaves
of each breath where the floating cormorants appear

and disappear, bluegills snap and flicker the surface
with enough flash to imitate
the long dead stars.
These are the nights the soul leaves the body to voyage
on its own. You have to see the universe as a living being

wrote Marcus Aurelius. It's as if those overlays of the body
in high school biology texts
revealed the stars.
Just so, infinity listens to the oceans trapped in conch shells
for assurances. We gaze into the skies of each other's eyes

to see what is beyond our seeing. The tide line's history
tells us all we need to know
of memory and loss.
It is like the silent echo of a bell buoy itself lost in the fog.
The man tracing the sands with a metal detector, the boys

searching for small treasures in the dunes, the lovers hoping
their footprints won't dissolve
with the rising tide,
the gulls poking through the sea froth, know what remains,—
this residue of love and desire that the heart salvages.

Now the lobster boats with their running lights have returned.
Some nights there is a phosphorus
glow that imitates
the Milky Way. We are all looking for words that wash up
like the smudged bottled messages from untold distances.

As a boy I used to keep starfish in pails of sea water so
they wouldn't crinkle like paper.
It was like carrying
my own universe within me. I imagined the land pirates
who lured fog bound ships onto the false harbor south of here

to wreck on the rocks for salvage. Only the Storm Petrels nesting
on the surface beyond the horizon
knew their truths.
They float in the midst of their own reflected universe that maps
the darkness below them. And us, if we stand there long enough

to realize it is we, too, who embrace the heavens, long enough
to follow our own footprints
leading off into
the dark beyond the town lights, we will find, if we see beyond
seeing, the shadows of the stars that long ago deserted us.

The Rivers

What happens in one place will happen everywhere
—Czesław Miłosz, *The Captive Mind*

When we turn away the river stops being the river.
Across it once the Cherokee were driven into exile
from this land where their dreams flew with the egrets,
and swam with the catfish, we are now squatters.
Tennessee, we say, a state and a river, but it's
Tanasi from two lost villages on its banks.
Now there are trucks hammering the bridge bolts
as they pass over carrying whatever seems important
to wherever their maps tell them to go. When you look
at yourself in the river you see how fragile you are,
torn apart by a ripple which is time passing through you
on its way to something larger. Parmenides thought
the world was made of water, but Plato knew it was
made of our dream of it. Our words always blur
the histories they name.
                              I remember studying my father's
Army Reserve maps, imagining troops moving across
the names of rivers and contour lines, creating a world
more real than any I'd known. It was as if I were
an aerial photographer but I could not, then, imagine
the scattered, shredded bodies. Even now I worry
what role I would have had. I can only hope the way starlight
dreams of darkness, the way darkness dreams of
the far edges of space. Our histories seem as unreal
as the images of Plato's cave.
                              Think of how in
Yuri Herrera's *Signs Preceding The End of The World,*
how his heroine is either passing over the Rio Grande
or passing into the ninth level of the Aztec underworld,
or both. And of Oscar Alberto Martinez Ramirez
and his 23-month-old daughter, Valeria, tucked inside
his T-Shirt, arm embraced around his neck where they both
washed up on the banks of the same Rio Grande, trying like
Herrera's heroine, like the lost Cherokee, to pass over.
They know that when one dream dies we all die.
Plato dreamt of the many suns that must be rising

on how many Planets. We send a probe to Pluto to see
how far our dreams will swim. How quickly we exile
the truth of love from the love of truth. It's true,
we look through a one-way mirror, but which way we don't know.

It wouldn't be long before my father's dreams crumpled
as did his visible world. We have to worry what our own
maps reveal, what current we follow.

                                    It wouldn't be long before
I tried to explain how the best way to see the mass graves
along the banks of the Jadar River in Bosnia was
by aerial photographs but whose real story was really
what we couldn't see—the genitals nailed to doors,
severed feet left frozen in the snow. It was not long
before I knew *that* world was not the world to live in.
Too many memories are inventories of the dark matter
of our world. If only the stars whose dust we began with
would still breathe inside us. Instead, a slow mist rolls in
from another age. The membranes of the soul begin to quiver.

My father knew that every map is a prayer, and every
prayer is a hope that this is not the world, but only
the terrors we have made of it, that we must learn
to map our lives as clearly as the stars we connect
into constellations, for we must all pass over
into a love whose future is all the future we have,
for it is the river that is sacred, as the Cherokee tell us—
a future, a place where the stars the river holds all night
wash up as cinders on some foreign shore, but only to be re-lit.

Elegy in a Storm

I'd see things no one else could see. . .
    —Stanley Plumly, "Brownfields"

All night the Luna Moth had circled the flickering
street light as if it were paying homage
to its own brief flash of life
while above, the moon itself seemed to waver

behind clouds of voile. You would have noticed,
then, the sudden sun's alarm lift a blanket
of crows from the Live Oak,
felt the air thicken, the wind start to tear the light

in the tree, the first pigeons confused to mumble
their philosophies, the mud daubers just
emerging from their tunnels
under the wilting side of the shed's roof, the screech

of a hawk's warning, as if he too could smell the rain
still far off where your clouds are testing
their shadows on the hillside.
What you wanted was the world we see, even though

the world we see is not the world we see, only
our memory in its imagining. It is not
the red and green screen shot
of the approaching storm on the cell phone,

a chameleon snake about the width of a county,
running north-south, shifting colors—
red, yellow, green,
almost autumnal, you'd say, sidling this way

with its future that may bring toppled trees and poles,
branches piecing the sides of the shed
like lances or battle axes,
enough of a metaphor for you to picture the man
sitting beside that shed in his fabric couch carried

from some distant, unknown place
by the storm, him holding
a birdcage, its two lovebirds singing anyway,

his own life scattered for miles, merging with other
missing lives, letters, bills, pictures,
families, what is beyond
this screen picture we save, as clear as the storm's snake,

though nothing tells us of the storm inside him,
nor in us watching, not understanding
what he feels, only
understanding that each breath we take we take with love.

A World without Angels Is Not a World

What is that world that appears behind the threads of our
firelight's flame unravelling in the infernal air, maybe
a vision of a few late buzzards harvesting abandoned shadows,
a world whose shadows ferry themselves across
the evening waters, shadows that blend with the bats
that skim the surface,
                              and what is that world that midnight
street cleaners wash away with the discarded prayers
of the day, where the steel crane lurking over the church
points to the river where the sandhill crane gazes
towards an empty future, a world of forgotten dreams
pooling in clogged gutters,—
                              aren't these the visions that reveal
to us the lonely hours of the soul, worlds where the open
mouths left on distant battlefields cry out to us? Above them
a few milkweed seeds pretend to float like angels.
The moonlight stretches its rope across the field.
Months later, a fleck of blood still stains a white rose.
Above it all, no angels, only the shredded clouds that
seem to have no place to go, a sunset that wants to
appear as an open wound.
                              My love, where are we?
what are we to do when all the reflections seem empty,
when the tent of stars seems to shroud the world,
when the only embraces seem to be given by shadows to
the shadows of shadows? For a moment, the pale, brooding
moon has no answer. Maybe hope is here, in the white ember
that suddenly comes alive.
                              Maybe, as the mystics pray,
we must drink the silence of the Angels believing
there is a world inside this one that flashes into being
the way those passing headlights light up the trees for
a moment which is more real than what the clocks have
ever measured, like a love that is invisible except
when it is not. So maybe Blake was right and we must

see eternity in that fleck of blood on the rose. "Brother
Sun, Sister Moon," Francis preached to the anxious birds,
for they, too, knew, like him, a world inhabited by Angels,
like the radio waves that pass through us unheard and
unseen, just as your radiant glance, even now, has lit up
those regions of the heart inaccessible by any map.

A Theory of Touch

For some of us there were many years of living past
Anyone we would have died for.
                                                    —Art Smith

As far as an elegy goes, your *canyon of the morning*,
that we all live in, will do. But, along that narrow creek
on the canyon floor, how do we measure the depth of its
shadows? It's like being in the little slit of consciousness
between our dreams.

                    A shaft of light blinding the canyon
walls prompts a hawk to suddenly lift from the cliff, leaving
its own shadow behind to follow its own dreams. In my dream,
there are newspapers with blank pages, maps with no place
names, words that will never be spoken, loves that have never
begun, vapor trails already frayed into ghosts of another time.

But what time? The past we try to create always creates itself
despite us. Its stars have faded because they have no choice.
The embers of last night's log collapse into themselves.
The watch's numbers move but have nothing to do with
its hours.

                    Is there no memory that remembers us? Even our
old photos have their own laments. They are like those two
ghost moons, balls of cosmic dust, circling earth, unseen
but for a polarizing lens. Or like the dust of the solar wind
that protects us from invisible cosmic rays. I want to think
that we are all part of some dust trailing forever from one
dream to the next. Or like the Northern Lights that seem
to beckon us towards whatever it is they signal from beyond.

There's no footpath here to follow, but further on the canyon
will widen into whatever it is going to be. In the distance
the walls seem to slant towards some unmapped floor.
The longer we walk the more we track an unseen dream.
It is as if one version of our dream touches another version.
It seems true, according to one theory, that every atom we touch

touches every other atom. The light first begins to touch what
it will illumine. Where we are begins to touch where we will be.
A few clouds have started to become their own shadows.
They are changing on the creek's surface that itself seems
to know what river or sea it will merge into. The wind holds
the flight of the hawk. Each breath holds another breath
inside it. We follow our own shadows by letting one word
touch another word, letting their shadows fall all around us
never so much alone, never so much a part of each other.

The Columbine: Terri in Her Garden

The silence within each word, the simple syntax of wind
whispered against the chimes, the owl's answers echoed
in the dark spaces dappling the immense, impossible sky
between stars, drifting as they have since the beginning,
everything becoming only what it will become, though
I could not have seen that in 1996 under the tree I still
can't name, nor most of the flowers you plant except
the red columbine, little lanterns lighting what we believe in,
the earth that returns what we give it, those transplanted
gardens of your dreams, the star that watches over
your face each night through the window, itself drifting
through time to disappear just as the morning doves
cloak the day's news, a world that hovers like the invisible
black holes that perforate the center of our galaxy,
what the untranslatable words of your sleep also cloak,
so that I should touch you as softly as that starlight did,
for it is true that every star wants to be the daylight,
every flower, every word wants to blossom the love
it harbors, showing a way like the light of your columbine
whose seeds will migrate next Spring into galaxies of color
we never expected, constellations that can whisper this love.

Elegy Just in Case

The end approaches, but the apocalypse is long lived.
        —Jacques Derrida, "Of an Apocalyptic Tone"

The river's down again, the boat piers loom
over the mud.
            An emptiness so vast I can't tell
if I am in it or it in me.
                As when I am barred
from my own dreams.
                Most of our lives we live
backwards. What I didn't say stalks me. What
I neglected waits in the trees with the vultures.

There are chasms in the words I have for this.
There is my old heart shuttered with denial.

It is as if the lost names rise now from the mud.

One of them arrives with his hands full of hours.
One arrives as a Luna moth at the back door.
Another knows his imagination contains his future.
Another, the eternity he dreams won't last for long.
Yet another, how we once walked on our knuckles.

On this starless night even the wind wants to be
visible.
        It is their dreams that have dropped anchor
in my own.
            As when the boy in Croatia marked
the poor stone grave with a simple prayer fingered
with the mud at his knees, and whose words
trembled with a flash of wind.
                    My own words are
dredging the river bed.
                The piers reach out towards
the trapped skiffs.
                What they search for is a time where
our dreams begin,

the river mud giving up its secrets,
stumps trying once again to be trees, a pair of boots
someone must have lost overboard before the drought,
the salamanders emerging, a few glistening stones
pretending to be islands,
                              the shadow of the heron
sweeping the surface, unable to find a proper ending.

Alone Together

Jean Valentine (1934 – 2020)

A far farm window shattered briefly into flame with the first
syllables of dawn,
                    "suppose we are standing together
for a minute," you wrote,
                                    and now, the scent of birdsong,
the sound of the rose op"ening like a whole note.
                                                    I mean
the way Bill Evans piano edges in as if careful not to break
the solitude, until Chet Baker's trumpet offers its tentative
support.
            You can feel the suspense like a hand on your shoulder.
What is the name for our name for that.
                                        So many pauses
in the music. If only we held the notes of our lives.
                                                        Earlier
I had been following the tracks of a lone deer, and the coyote's
careful, stalking prints over them.
                                    Now, listening to Herbie Mann's
flute arriving to tell us we are always alone, I wonder if the God
you felt near the "River at Wolf" is what Baker, too, searches for.

Did the deer reach the swamp, or the bramble further down trail?

"You will always have to live in doubt," the song ends.
                                                "Our second life,"
you wrote as if in reply, the way the earth rotates, almost unheard.

Quantum Entanglement

Reality is the persistent illusion.
—Einstein

For Pam and Bill

St Francis knew the birds he preached to were also the souls
of those that scratched the sky above him in Giotto's fresco.

The world is full of alternate histories, wrote Richard Feyman.

Time hums in the background like the cicadas that start, stop,
and echo one another from one end of the woods to another.
Or like those fireflies that synchronize themselves in waves
that drift back and forth through the trees like the Northern Lights.

That's why the clock's hands always point away from the center,
why the further we look deeper into the night sky the closer we get
to when we began.
                              That's why Francis' stigmata is echoed in
the five stars of Cassiopeia who was placed there for believing
she was, as one story has it, more beautiful than her sea nymphs.
While the tide rises on one shore it pulls away from the other.

It's always five o'clock somewhere someone says, raising a glass
to the invisible stars. In this way, one world, one meaning, leaks
into another that never suspects it. In the fifth grade I dressed
as Francis for the school pageant which was, for a time, my own
reality. That was the year Bernie Doyle died, though he still exists
in a few earlier poems, and now, again, here.
                              Maybe everything is
a symbol for what it could be. The plastic of this computer is made
from the oil which came from the decayed bones of what?—a fern,
a dinosaur, some ancient hominid noticing a supernova above him?

Aren't we always, as our daydreams wander, in two places at once?
Each world appears as suddenly as the volunteers, the unexpected
plants that keep on coming to light like new stars in my wife's
compost garden. Each time we embrace we embrace all that we have
been, all that we might become, everyone who is a part of us.
Quantum entanglement is what the scientists call it, which is also
the way we love what is not there as much as we love what is.

Was

There are atoms, and the spaces between them;
surmise makes up the rest.
                    —Democritus

Wind without air. Stars with no sky. Matter that is empty space.

Some science says the universe is just bits of information.

Wherever you are is not where you are. Your world is the mirage
you make it to be. Sometimes it is the sinkhole that opens
beneath us.

          How can we know what is real? These are speculations
that hide truth like leaves covering the surface of the pond.

Still, far traffic whines about the hill, the coffee's on, the paper's
delivered, birdsong has begun to find its way out of the woods,
and soon the new hay bales begin to smudge the air with their
yellow light.

          We know a new particle by a trail it leaves
on film. We know a new planet by the periodic dip in its star's
brightness as it orbits in front of it. The music of the spheres is
how the Greeks explained it.

                    We never see the drone's work
until we hear we bombed the village orphanage to save the village.
The combat aerial photographer never sees the close-up.

For years my friend checked the perimeter windows of his house
and slept in his kitchen cabinet for fear of the enemy ghosts still
slipping out of the jungle.

                    Wherever we are is wherever we dream.

There's a solar wind that blows stellar dust across the galaxies
From billions of years ago in constellations that exploded like cluster
bombs in a sky that has long since disappeared.
                         According to some
geometries you can travel in a straight line and start over again where
you began well before you began. It's the only hope we have.

Elegy with No Real Ending

For my student, Jane Bradley

Tonight, from down between the two ridge lines
the scream of a Great Horned Owl who must have
seized some rabbit whose high-pitched scream cut
through the night.
                It was all over before I returned.

Sometimes our lives flutter like the Luna Moth
arguing with the streetlight.
                Sometimes we can
sense what Stevens called *"the odor of stars"*
that links us to whatever is beyond us.
                Tonight now,
listening to Benny Golson's elegy for Clifford Brown
in Dizzy's version from before either of us breathed
air, I think of how Brownie, too, was gone so
unexpectedly.
                It's the way each chord seems to extend
itself that makes it so mournful. It's the way the solo
trumpet tries to rise above its own lament that says what
I could not invent a word for when I heard the news.

I remember how you mourned in class at Darwish's
poem, "Identity Card," and its sad music. How much of
what we lose is dimly echoed in what we write or hear.

In the end, Dizzy brings us back to where we began.

I think tonight of resurrection ferns saving their water
while the others died away, or the woodpecker walking
headfirst down the trunk as if to defy gravity, and the tiny
squirrel stretched out like a snake to get at the bird feeder,
the opossum sheltering its young in the tangled branches
of the fallen oak after the storm, these things that struggle
to continue with everything else that lives on the next page.

Still, to think of a world is not the same as having it.
From between the ridges, every yelp and whine
reminds us how delicate the world is. Each note
for Clifford arrives as if from nowhere and heads
uncertainly into its own future.
                              "I don't want this poem
to end,," Darwish once wrote. But it always does.

WHERE THE WIND COMES FROM

(2021)

Prologue: Litany from Before the Beginning

The work is the origin of the artist.
            —Heidegger, "The Origin of the Work of Art"

From the dark flower of the black hole desiring to embrace us.
From our galaxy that shudders to shed us after each war.
From the invisible planet we know by its gravity.
From our brittle lives that break apart on moonlight.
From the sirens that slice through the scarves of night.
From the girl shot through her bedroom wall in a drive-by.
From a blink tangled in the eels of the nervous system,
the creeping whispers of the Morning Glory, the solace
of the passerby who places a blanket under the victim's
head, from a man on the streetcar hawking day old
newspapers, and the hawk itself riding sleeves
of wind, from the cemetery wall that fails to keep
death in and the child's first breath that lets death
escape. Everything containing its opposite.
From the unspoken or repressed words of the prophets.
From the mothers uncovering the mass graves
in Srebeniča, Argentina, Berundi, Salvador.
From the lover whose skin ripples at a touch
and whose enormous heart could rival the Killer
Whale's which weighs over a ton. From the smell of
fresh rain on the blacktop roads to galaxies collapsing
into grains of light. Everything exploding into the shape
of hymns. From our lives like jet trails or a father
blowing smoke rings in the shape of mother's rosary.
From the soldier surprised at how easily the bullet tore
through his flak jacket as he disappeared into
jungle shadows. From the homeless woman
on the subway, her life brimming over her tattered
shopping bags. From Time sweating through the walls
and pipes of our hopes. From the protesters marching
in the streets and across bridges. From the beheadings
that blaspheme the name of God, but also the man
reciting the poem at the poet's grave for he knows
the nightshade has its own time for flowering.

From orchards and tenements, from cloudbursts
and droughts, from lichen, highways, waterfalls,
from the dogwood trying always to straighten itself,
from the new species of ourselves unearthed in Africa,
from Love itself, her knees pulled up, her face glowing
in firelight, her favorite sickle moon cutting a new trail
across the sky, and from our words like heart, like soul,

like prayer, from wonder, from forgiveness,
from everything that knows our love before we do.

Cain's Legacy

You can't stop the boxcars of despair.
You can't stop my voice from hiding out
like a virus inside your words, their knives
clamped between your teeth. You can't stop
the dogs gnawing on the bones from mass graves.
Thus your mirrors holding other faces. Thus your lungs
filled with someone else's words.
The eyelids of the heart closing. The sky drunk
on vapor trails. Otherwise, a few packages of conscience
to the refugees. You can't stop the sounds
of exploding stars as they approach you.
The anxious triggers. The land mines of idealism.
You can't stop Dismay from stumbling
out of the trenches of your dreams.
You can't stop these ghosts sitting around your table
gnawing on the past. Their candles burn down
to shimmering wounds in their cups.
Everyone holding their favorite flags like napkins.
The sound of bugles spilling from the room like laughter.
I know, you kill what you love just to hate yourself
all the more. You put on the cloak of distance.
A wind that blows away the weeks. The lovers' wilted embrace
that was your only, your last hope.
Everyone his own Judas. After a while
even the moon is just an excuse not to look too closely.
You can't stop the past boiling up in the heart like lava.
Otherwise, a history written by shadows.
For example, someone says the universe is expanding,
more anxious optimism, but where would it expand into?
There's only the vacuum that's always inside us.
There's Stephen Hawking saying the past is pear shaped
but that doesn't feed anyone. You can't stop the brain
of the starving child turning into a peach pit,
not his body terrorizing itself for food,
not his face wrinkling like the orange you leave on your table,

his liver collapsing, the last few muscles snug
over his bones like the tight leather gloves of your debutante.
Otherwise your old lies yawning to wake in the corner.
You can't stop the pieces of the suicide bomber
from splattering all over the cafe walls.
You can't stop the walls the tanks crush from rising again.
Otherwise a few tired rivers, a few fugitive stars.
The seasons that ignore us. The cicadas giving up on us.
Hope's broken antennas. Love trying to slip out of the noose.
The betrayed lives we were meant to live.
You can't stop that town from turning its soul on a spit,
not the light chiseling away desire, the morning
wandering dazed through the underbrush of deception.
You can't stop these sails of tomorrow hanging limp
from their masts. All you have are these backwaters of touch,
this voice spinning like a broken compass,
this muzzle made from your own laws.
But you can't stop the bodies piling up.
You can't stop the deafening roar of the sky.
You can't stop the bullet you've aimed at your own head.

The Secret Word: Lot's Wife

How could anyone not look back? Not even darkness
could have closed my eyes. I became the salt
of the earth, as your saying goes. But Lot never even
noticed me the next day. Salt of the earth. How could
anyone? The sun rose as usual. Cities shimmered
in the distance. I stood there like Eurydice as the earth
exploded. The sand is there only to explain the wind.
The hills ignore the valleys. The moon disowns its own
origins. The only life we have is history. But you are
afraid to look at your own past, your massacres for
your god or country, the hungry you ignore, the land
you kill. Salt of the earth. Next year's moths are waiting
in cocoons you nurtured yesterday. Who is anyone without
a desire to see what happens? You fill your clocks with
pictures that are out of focus. Everything you do provokes
the stars. That is why their cryptic alignments refuse
to give warnings. And the one word you have tried all
your lives to say dies on our lips as you die. It blows away
with the desert sand. Why do you believe your own words?
When was it your own Jesus called his disciples
the salt of the earth? My own names are on parole.
You turn your histories into anecdotes or slogans.
The horizon has crumbled. The weight of the sky is
nearly unbearable. All your signposts are blank.
The rags of forgotten flags litter your fathers' lands.
Your truth is what you believe, but it is only a distorted
carnival mirror. That's why there is always that unwanted
stranger, who looks away, lurking behind the subjects of
your photos. He steals the scene the way I steal your thoughts.
You say peace but mean war, love but mean power.
In the end you will forget your own names. Some
scribes have called me Edith. You can look it up.
It is just a word, and of no consequence. History says
I should warn you, and have. There. As if it would do
any good. Like me you'll turn and look. Like I did
you'll see only what you want to see, name only
what you want to name. Salt of the earth.

Moses' Revision

You shall remember that you were an alien
In the land of Egypt, therefore I am
Commanding you to do this thing.
        —Deut 24:21-22

I was always an illegal alien. I never knew God.
For some I was an Egyptian, for others an outsider,
for others a Hebrew. Who ever knows who they are?
Our stories are the myths that seem to write themselves:
I won a war by holding up my arms, or split the seas.
In truth, I was a victim of my own stories. I killed a man,
a guard, because I thought of the man he was beating
as a brother. In the desert there are voices everywhere.
The sound of light as it bakes the earth, stars scuffing
the sky, water whispering not far beneath our feet.
Yesterday's clouds leave their thumbprints on the sky.
Everything is a metaphor. Our lives are metaphors.
The sun rises on a pillar of light. The birds arrive before
dawn with their secret messages. Everything is a mystery:
water from rocks, bushes that speak through their flames.
What can you do but believe? For all I did, I doubted
only once. Another time He tried to kill me for forgetting
who I am, just one soul among the souls of the earth.
His ways are Hi ways. It's like trying to explain why
He lets the moon blot out the sun. In the end, I wrote
what I saw but never understood. I was wrong.
What I took for an enemy was a mirage. It was we
who invaded. It was we who came in on the migrant wind.
Now you think you know what I meant, but your own words
cast endless shadows. Everyone has their Golden Calves.
You hoard yours behind the darker walls of your hearts.
You would have cast me back across your borders.
We were all migrants then, we are all migrants now.
I have my visions and now my revisions. We were chosen not
to destroy but to reveal, to warn. A handful among the grains
of the earth, a galaxy among the stars. In the end I cursed
some of you, but that, too, was wrong. We curse ourselves,
yet I see now, beyond the land I could not enter, the far lands
you have made: shadows without bodies, black holes for souls.

David's Lost Psalm

Winter's net of black branches has begun to haul in
a few buds and leaves. There's nothing to explain
our desire to embrace all that surrounds us. A sudden
sun has made the statues glisten. "I was the man,"
as Nathan said, which proved a burden. I remember
my own age of cries as dreadful as yours. We all desired
a story different than the one we lived. I sang
whatever was true, however painful or torturous,
not to dwell in those valleys but to climb out of them.
No one wanted to remember the wars, the captivity,
the rapes. No one wanted to remember that we too
did unspeakable crimes. Now your own stories are
so light they drift away like milkweed looking for
some better ground. There isn't any, there never is.
The moon's scarred face gives us back our souls.
Saul thought I would drift away, then tried to kill me.
I forgave him as I forgave myself. Or wanted to.
Each act leaves a footprint neither the wind nor
the sea can sweep away. My own faults now
crumble like pages of a forgotten passion.
You must think of me as a predator. This is why
I sing, as a much a dream as song. All I know is
that memory is a place that is nowhere, which is why
we can retrieve the lives we never lived. Each song is
a woods where the paths return always to the beginning.
I sing to invent what I can not remember, or to remember
what I can not invent. It is the only way to let my soul
glisten as if it knew. Here a few deer step out of the woods.
The cornstalk stubble has been burnt away. The cemetery
stones are telling only a part of the story but that seems
enough. A sudden wind nudges the statues awake.

Nathan: Speaking Truth to Power

In truth, his great heart was a weathervane.
He followed the faded tracks of illusory animals,

mistook frost crystals for stars, reflections over
the things themselves. No leader is a leader

who sends a man alone to the front lines in order
to claim his widow. You have to say something.

I told him the story of the rich man claiming
the flock of the poor, but what I meant was him.

Who did that, he asked. *You are the man,* I said.
Then the wind shaped a hand slapping his face.

And you, what truths have you said or done?
Your own kings have stories like clouds of locusts.

Their words create endless box canyons.
Their words are mudslide covering whole villages.

You have to speak from where the wind comes from,
to risk your words falling like stones into the river,

before you appear like a mirage on the desert floor,
before your own words become homeless, your

shadows misshapen, and before you, too,
are deported into a language you no longer speak.

Micah's Prophecy

Time subsides and you fall back into the hammock
of another easy truth. There are so many ways to
disguise this. One reigning idea dictates what you will
think, and so you go blundering from one war to another,
one rape or abuse to another. My dream for you is clothed
with shadows. Listen, your final dawn will arrive rudely.
What became of me wasn't worth the telling. But, I'll say
this: the real dungeons are our own words, the real chains
are the ones we use to encircle our own hearts. There are
letters in my alphabet you'll never know. I saw a whole
army collapse like a huge lung. I saw bodies fall like
chips from a woodsman's axe. There was a king who
believed me, and one who didn't. You know their fates.
Your own king's pencil in their beliefs for later erasure.
After each tragedy they hand out antique apologies.
"Thoughts and prayers," you say, echoing an empty cavern.
Your mouths have the shapes of the end of a muzzle.
Your eyes are gunsights, your ears are petrified wood.
Someone shoots in a theater and soon it plays like fiction.
Someone else pulverizes symbols they don't understand.
When you break the world it doesn't just get fixed.
You have no idea how many things you've become
a symbol for. Your answers explode like terrorist bombs.
There is a truth, if you listen, but it arrives with no
postmark and no return address, no provision for revision.
Even your windows mutter things you refuse to understand.
I can say: there is little patience with your skeletal words.
I can say: you should already know this by reading
what has already been written on the dungeon walls of
your own hearts and the watermarks of your own souls.
The harp plays on, but the question is, who's listening?

Elijah's Warning

Why does the soul, a startled dove, flee from itself?
Why do we live so often in the dark caves of the heart?
These are the questions that nest like a tangle of spiders.
A man rises from the subway vent to a world that has
abandoned the world—to draw his lost life over a billboard
picture of a life he'll never know. Listen, there are storms
that shred mountains. There are rocks that shake themselves
as the earth splits. There are my words that you burned
to ashes now floating aimlessly. No one wanted to listen.
How easy it is to hope the clouds wash away the sky's light.
We have become so inventive in our cruelties—as today
a flash of shrapnel flies through a hospital ward, someone
drives a car into a crowd, an ISIS sniper welcomes the challenge
of a child's small head, another child is hollowed out by
a gang bullet from beyond her bedroom wall. No one wants
to listen. Ages ago I told the king what would happen.
Now, I'm telling you: your own kings are leading you
to dreams that are not dreams with words that are not words,
hopes that are not hopes. No one seems to understand
the shimmer of light that surrounds you before the lightning
strikes. Your excuses rise from the trees like vultures. No one
understands the script for their own roles drawn on abandoned
walls. But there's no language, no image that won't tell you what
I mean. Listen to the pain of the hills as they are torn apart
for a few dollars and whose veins are piped with poisons. Listen
to the cry of the child caught in the rubble of a suburban meth lab.
Listen: you have to hear more than you can hear. You can't really
understand until you hear the weight of pollen as it falls to earth,
the sound the moon makes dragging its pale, almost invisible
light, across the daytime sky the way you push the air apart as you
walk, which is the soul's breath leaving or entering, which is
your breath as it sifts through the caves of your lungs. Listen.

Ruth's Advice

Did it matter if my blood was streaked like one of
those streams that stumble by our broken world?
I stepped into the field like a field until he nearly
tripped over me. You know nothing of real solitude—
your stories and your mirrors keep you company.
Why can't you go wherever your love goes, live
wherever your love lives? If you are going to love
you have to be ready to sacrifice everything. I could have
returned to comfort in Jerusalem, not lived among
those people I hardly knew. I loved all that I loved.
I worked everything that needed to be worked:
It wasn't my grain but what that grain could mean.
In the end all our lives are strewn across the road
like curls of one of your truck's blown tires.
What's to salvage? Look around us all now.
Sometimes we don't even know what you thirst for.
We think we can give yourself over to the wind.
Don't you think the bed sheets scorched my skin?
I lay at Boaz' feet and, startled, he covered me. I put
my mouth to his heart. The night tilted away from us.
I became one of you. You became one of me. But
I never understood how you could hang someone's words
like a man from a tree, or just even refuse someone
a place to sit. In the long run it leads to the way we can
refuse the women in Darfur raped by the Junjaweed,
Devils on Horseback. And the children, thousands,
chased by government planes that slash the skin of the sky,
armored jeeps in a country that is a storm of vultures,
a chain of coffins. Each time we turn away we bruise
our own souls. Each time we turn away our own death
drifts like fallout through our hearts. What do we want?
Where are we if we can't love the worst of us?
What are we if we can't try to mend the dusk's bleeding sky?
What are we if we can't love more than the world allows,
more than the odor of fig trees that fills the night air,
more than the late swallows that circle, embracing the last tree?

Job's Epilogue

The stars prowled my skin but all I wanted
in the end was to see His face. I never doubted
when the rivers that I knew as Him dried up.
Why did H want to stay so hidden? Blake says
you can see Him in every grain of sand. There is
a million-mile-high tornado wandering through
the Lagoon galaxy that might be Him. There are
these icicles reaching desperately for the earth
that may also be Him. Now all I see is an old man
called Death standing under the storefront light
across the street clipping his nails. Does it matter?
All love turns into a beetle in the end. You have
to crush the shell with your heel to survive.
My own friends were a broom to any hope.
They watched me pass through time like a body
caught under the thickening ice until Spring.
They tossed their words like salt on my garden.
They called themselves allies but they were planting
the explosives of revenge like terrorists.
They thought every sickness was a sin.
They thought they could cloak their own guilt
in words that surrounded me like clouds of insects.
They wanted to grab my soul by its throat.
Now they are rolling up your field maps,
looking for a destiny shaped like a conquerable
country, shaped even like the Afghan boy
whose hands have been cut off for stealing
food, like the girl nailed to the door in Bosnia.
Their words siphoned the air around me until
there was only stone. I could see the moon
turn its back to me. I could see the empty trains
leaving the camps, the minefields sprouting
like newly planted crops. They wanted to leave me
lying dead on my own body. My soul was
playing tug of war with the wind. There was never

any meaning to any of it was what the beetles knew.
I'm not saying you don't have any choice but
we get poured out like milk, then thicken like curds.
In the end, all we can drink are our own regrets.
If we were pieces of straw we'd be hunted down.
Their armies are toppling minarets and burning churches.
What good is it to let our thoughts burn like a naked
bulb in the prisoner's room? Eternity has a few more
words to say. I have more than I ever had, but less.
I could see the birds falling from my trees like leaves.
I could see my cup filling with shadows. I could see
the sun was only another kind of cage. What did
He think I would do with all I saw? Hope put away
its watch. Whenever I asked, His ears were full
of darkness. He thought I wanted to harness the stars.
He thought I wanted to teach the grasshopper to leap.
All I wanted in the end was to see His face. You can
hear each new idea rumbling over the horizon. It is written
somewhere that I am each one of you, that the moths
of despair have eaten away our desires, that our hopes
have turned to scar tissue and harden, but it isn't true.
We have to understand the sunlight as a way to cast shadows.
We have to touch each other's shadows like our own.
We have to understand each heart is a kind of cave.
We have to let the bats of hatred fly out of those caves.

Jeremiah's Lament

They said my voice was the storm that gathers in the flower.
They said my words covered the fields like locusts.
Whatever they said, I never wanted to stand apart, even
when they buried me under stones shaped from their hearts.
Yes, midnight clung to my lips, yes inside my mouth the stars
trembled, but who really listened? All they heard was
their own guilt crying inside them like caged birds.
Did what I say come true? Evil lurked in their wells.
God picked them clean the way a shepherd picks his cloak
clean of vermin. In the end, they gasped for air like jackals.
And truth in all this? You yourself have your physics
for the world,—quarks, for example, a matter of
mere logic to some, a real image to others. It only matters
that you believe. You have your own histories
strangling you like vines. For instance, 1597: the year
of the first military field hospitals, the year Spain
and France began peace talks, or the year Samurai warriors
brought back barrels filled with 100,000 noses and ears
from Korea to Kyoto. In Mostar they are still digging under
the rubble of someone's false prophecy. They are looking
for the truth that bursts from a hand grenade. We listen
only to history's megaphone, not the words that splinter
on whispers. We are all turning on a potter's wheel
that shapes one ethnic cleansing after another.
I wanted common words that would laugh and weep at once,—
the fig trees that ripen as the mountains tremble,
the wolves of our desire whose voice flowers in the forest.
But these are the words that put me in jail, words
that lashed my own back, that seared my eyes, words that
still nest in the desert cactus. You call it beautiful, but
the song of the nightingale is only the pain
of never finding its own voice. Still,
everything speaks if you listen closely enough:
the desert dunes sing and moan, shout and stammer
under the weight of their own shifting sands, bees

make a map of air currents by beating their wings.
And my dreams? I dreamt God's judgment
in an almond rod, the city as a boiling pot, and I am
still waiting to see what they mean. I was
promised a bronze-walled city to protect me.
I was promised that the doors of Love would fly open.
Foggy with desire, we have to make our own truths.
All I can tell you is how it is your most precious Hope
that catches on the brambles, that blooms with each rain.
Imagine the stars filling the bottom of your glass.
I swear to you, the sun surrendering itself to darkness
beyond the tree line is the most poignant of moments.

Hosea's Appeal

*Therefore the land mourns, and all who live in it languish;
together with the wild animals and the birds of the air,
even the fish of the sea are perishing.*
                              —Hosea 4:3

If you would listen, you could hear
the White-Brown Sparrow Weavers
sing duets so precise their brains work
as one, like the partners they are. You
can see them resting on the fence rail
that is pushed up like the arthritic back
of an old man, or from a branch that leans
down as if to whisper its own warnings
to the earth. But you have to look, and
you have to listen. This, too, is a vision
beyond sight. Know that they only sing in
your disappearing wild, not in the world
you have rusted like your iron cities.
The lost elms were a warning. The beautiful
red sky that opens its hands to you
in the morning comes not from itself
but the billion particles that poison it.
I can tell you now: you are smelting
your own hearts, your souls. But those
birds, their sounds translate the sounds
of stars at a pitch you can never hear.
Even your physics tells you every atom
sings to every other atom. That's
a parable you haven't really learned.
You could have read it in Humbolt.
You could have read it in Blake—
Everything that Lives is Holy.
When you see the moon scarred
by the broken branches of a tree
take it as a warning. When you see
a star burning out, remember
the retreat of forests into the desert.
When you mistake the horn of a truck
for the song of a bird, it is already over.

Junia's Name

—Rom. 16:7

It begins with a mustard seed and then you have
a twenty-foot tree spreading out like a pinwheel
galaxy. With me it was centuries before they translated
my name as a woman. *I is another*, Rimbaud once wrote.
In place of me they needed a mcause Paul
called me his fellow apostle and prisoner. It's like
someone dialing your number but insisting
your name is wrong. The tears are centuries old.
They look at the stars and invent their own constellations.
They don't see we are slowly devouring the dwarf galaxy
in Sagittarius while some other galaxy hunts us.
All that will be left will resemble a burnt-out haystack.
The low music of the cosmos will grow fainter.
But for now we are like the lost notes on an abandoned
guitar. Sometimes they like to think of us like those
No-see-ums that plague you. How many times
have our ideas wilted on their vines before they blossom?
Their words float by like tumbleweed, their histories
read like unmarked dirt roads. I am not sure how
to explain all this. There are worlds inside us
they will never know, like the Light that bends
so much we never know where it came from.
It hardly knows what to do with their world. Its stars
meditate on the origin of darkness. It is a history
you will have to write. But for now we are
like pages torn from a book. The search for
our history is the search for the soul. Be patient.
It took ages to rise from the sea. The sun leaves
both shadows and Light. You have to wait by moving.
You have to let the wind erase your footprints.
There are roads not visible on your maps. Pascal
thought the world was a funhouse where we become
an insect in one mirror, a giant in another. We are never
where we are. How often are we only metaphors
for what we want to be. I can tell you that what we take

to be stars are galaxies, and what we take as galaxies
are the thumbprints of God. But that is not what you want
me to say, to condemn their name for me. Just wait.
Time stammers by but says little we understand.
Everything is bigger than it is. All their words have never
changed the weather, nor will it change us.
They hold up babies and give speeches to faded
gravestones. They control the pronouns in a language
whose meaning holds little for us. They are the dark
spaces between constellations. Their souls wait for
the history like a deaf host waiting for his guests
to write down the meaning of their silences. See:
their words are beginning to fill each moment with
their own emptiness, their dreams wander through
darkened streets. The stars they thought the lake held
for them each night are already washing up on the shore.

Thomas' Blindness

That was years ago, a time when flocks of gulls
seemed to flap through my head. Everything was
its own promise. But what was really there?
The future seemed to explode
like one of your mortar shells. The vines flowered
briefly but no squash appeared. All that Spring,
the insects were questioning my face.
I could hear the bones of brush clatter in the wind.
With these fingers I pulled back the folds of His wound
like a billfold. I should have believed. It is hard
to believe our words that tell us only what took place
in the past. Now as I walk through the words for field,
for mountain, let the word for moonlight shift
among the orange trees, the word for shadow lean
like a hobo against the rocks, how could I know
what they meant to do? How they meant not
field but emptiness, not mountain but distance,
not moonlight or shadow but hope and despair.
It is our own guilt the dogs sniff out along the roadside.
Who led me to these cliffs or where I should go,
I can't say, but I can dream the town below,
the streets orderly as fishnet, the women
whose fat hangs from their arms loose
as the bellies of clams. I know, but can't see
how moonlight chalks the water.
How either silt pours from the river or
the eels are running again,
how shells of boats barnacle the beach, wishbones
the seas in winter broke. Even now, there are
these little blisters of sound that reach my ears.
For instance, the gulls that pester returning boats
like moths around a light. And there is
that sound of shovels
scraping against bone as they dig up
the graves of the victims no one believed from Kosovo.

Old enough to confuse dream and eyesight, I'm afraid
that my own dream might also fail
or that it include someone known
washing in the surf like seaweed. Will that be me
dreaming my life? I can feel the backhand of the light
brush over my face or maybe it is a dream
like His voice that burrows, still, into the cliffside.
Our sins start with something as invisible as lice.
The years are forgotten notes that slip from our pockets.
It is time to read those notes. It is time
to listen for the echoes of what you once believed,
a time still shivering in the trenches.
The time He took, the time He made more real.

The Apology of Judas

In those days I could fold the sky up and store it
in a closet. With every heave of my chest
the universe seemed to expand. In those days
the rope of the moon floating on the surface
of the water was a kind of hope. I hardly noticed
the bird's song limping from its broken nest,
hardly noticed the last star struggling against
the dawn until the sun betrayed it. Why do
we notice so little? Does the river suffer when
you plunge your hand into it? Does the wind suffer
when it snags itself on a branch? Maybe that's why
we close our eyes to kiss. I think each night was just
the bandage I used to cover the deep cuts of His words.
Don't turn away. Don't imagine you know the story.
Our lives are just dreams someone sold to the
highest bidder. I thought my own words could
trample the stars. I thought my name would nest
in the future and take flight. But there was only
that dusk of blackbirds. It's all just Fate settling
like dust in the attics of our deeds. But why
were they surprised? Why was a sword drawn?
Why has a sword always been drawn? Why do we
turn away from all those bodies of children bulldozed
into Bosnia, or the nursing mothers whose breasts are
cut off with machetes in Liberia just to deny the future?
Maybe we have to betray ourselves in order
just to be ourselves. In the end, Truth taps
at the windows of our souls. What quivers on the lake
are only the footprints of Fate. Even our astronomers
hear the funeral sounds of dying galaxies before they
ever see them. Gusts of time are filling my lungs.
They all said I was just a small part of the plan,
that they hold no grudges, no plans for revenge.
Then why is there such a haze over my heart?
I'm the crow the hawks chase from their nests.

I used to think Love would protect us from the shadows
we cast. I used to think that Hope was not what
jingled in our pockets. I used to think all this loneliness
would be unbearable. Now each word is a betrayal,
is the frayed rope-end of desire. Everything I say is
like some cargo hidden in the hold of a sunken ship.
In the end we all learn there's no sea, no sky, no word
big enough to hold all our pain. Only this kiss. Only
Love's dragline already hooking the very thing it fears.

Mary's Parable

Every morning the sun paused over the hills
as if it too knew what I wasn't ready to see.
Even then, each memory was a path crossing another
path like a fish net that captures only the passing currents.
Those mornings the shadows birds passed over me
carrying away so many moments that will never return.

What would you have done if you knew the end?
Who could really understand what it all meant?
What mother would not try to delay the passing
of seasons, not try to pluck the thorns from the rose?

But His words still hang in the air like the valley fog.
It is true, they hold so much that is unspoken. Like
the way it's impossible to describe the light as it
flexes across the desert's surface, or the way night
shadows seem more real than what they seem to image.

So too, it was only later that His words bloomed,
only later that I understood each story He told hid
a story that we are still trying to learn. What hurts
more than that story is what it has become for you.
It is not for you to pick the single bits and pieces
of what He said that suit the way you want to live.
You have to cast about your past. You were not
made in the image you have become. Each one
of you should be Him, but for you the homeless
are invisible, the poor cast aside like the lepers
of my own day. Your hungry live from dumpster
to dumpster. You slap your enemies with lies
and bombs. Surely, there is no one you love
more than yourselves.
                              I could go on, but let me
tell you a story: one morning I made my way

through the olive groves, the ground fog rising
nearly to the tops of the trees. I could hear, not see
the birds awaken, could almost hear the heat rising
from the dirt, could taste the rain that was about
to arrive, feel the light stroking my hands as
the fog lifted. I think the whole world held me
in its invisible, impossible arms, as if to say
we are all one, a mystery each sun tries to reveal.

BROKEN HORIZONS

(2018)

Easy

A few constellations begin to poke through the fabric
of the sky. Bits of moonlight rub against the water.
It's easy to imagine how the leftover light at dusk
leaves us wandering through our own dreams
trying to pick out what's real. It's easy to see
the man at the railing of the Walnut Street Bridge as
a jumper. Just think of the way his lost past sits like
a squatter on his heart, how whatever he dreamt
has gone on without him. Is that why he has tossed
a few coins in the sax player's case? Nightbirds in
the trestle above him keep repeating things he can't
say himself. There's the mold in the fridge, the shadeless
lamp. You can imagine the rest. There's always a note
someone's saved.
           Do you think I am making this up because
it's so easy? It may be that our words colonize our feelings,
that we know everything by its opposite. *"Why is there
something rather than nothing?"* the philosophers always ask.
We really can't escape what we dream. I wish I could
know if the man were going to jump, but what would I do?

I've come here to listen to the music, not to write this.
Words have their own agenda and it doesn't include us.
So it's easy to see how our histories get lost the way
those plastic bags that were once filled with items we've
long forgotten accumulate against the chain link fence.
Each star we can name is surrounded by its own darkness.
There's the river's darkness in every history we know.
Not so many years ago they hung two Black men,
Ed Johnson in 1906 and Alfred Blount in 1893 on this
bridge continuing, as it were, after Columbus who
enslaved and let be raped, over a quarter million
Taino Indians in Hispanola. And now they are
uncovering another mass grave in Mexico, more
in the Sudan, opening like trap doors to the soul,

and it would be easy to file that away and write about
something personal and forget everything that's happened.
It's easy to stand by like the bystanders who recorded
the assault on Gilbert Estrada, aged 51, in San Diego
on their cell phones. In truth, they hovered over
their own shadows.
          There's a hive of stars gathering
above the bridge. I would like to find the words
to make sure the man only looks longingly at the way
night has begun to deepen itself in the river. It's easy
to drown yourself in words that drift out of your past.
"Don't play what's there, play what's not there,"
Miles Davis once said. And maybe that's the answer.
We have our Being in others, Paul Tillich wrote.
When a fish splashes the water with light we want
to take it as a sign.
          I've said about all I can.
I'll keep watch until the Bridge is cleared.
Venus has sunk below the far hill. *'Round Midnight*,
the sax player starts up again just to keep breathing.
Our own lives are littered with darkened voices.
"Why Was I Born?" played Kenny Burrell and John Coltrane,
and the night blows over. It's a question you have
to answer on the bridge. It's not easy, but it's up to you.

Invisible Star Maps

Remembering my stepdaughter, Kari Harvey (1982 – 2016)

We know that we have passed out of death into life.
—1 John 3:14

Wherever we go we leave a thumbprint of the soul.
Ghosts of words we never said fill the rooms we leave.
This is why we have to touch what the missing have touched.
In the morning we see how the orb weaver has mapped
the last light, and how the Gazania flower opens its colors
to morning.

The heart maps these stories where the clocks
seem unsure of themselves.

Now the heron lifting suddenly
from the shore leaves the story I need to write. I believe
these things the way the tree believes in the dark world
of its roots, or how the brook remembers its origins upstream,
how we know where we are by the clang of a buoy through fog.

The heart maps invisible traces that are fog on my eyeglasses.
What we don't see is, in the end, the shore we are headed for.

Medieval map makers drew what might happen at each turn
on their journey, or made perfect picture worlds that existed
only in myths because they knew every place is a storehouse
of possibility, every place is a time that has yet to occur,
an unreadable history of the heart. In Syria the smudges
on aerial photographs are the mass graves of the missing.

The heart maps paths the survivors still take through abandoned
minefields. What we don't hear is, in the end, the distant rumor of dawn.

In the nineteenth century spectral photos returned the dead
to us. Now, just these old Polaroids, snapshots of some family
gathering. If only they could show me what lies beyond us.
Strabo (64BC-24AD) traced his spherical star maps

onto his earth map to bring us closer to heaven. Opicicni drew
his mystic world as graffiti on city walls, the Mediterranean
here as queens, saints, gryphons and other mysteries to be explored.

The heart maps the empty sky between those constellations.

It's true that all these facts are ways to avoid my own losses,
as if history erased the many histories it is made of.

What we don't see is, in the end, what the stars are hiding.

We want to put ourselves into the maps our dead have followed.
We want to read the elusive messages the wind writes
with ocean spray. We want to see heaven pivot on its axis
with every memory that breaks the surface. Here the moon
drags the dawn behind it. Eternity hides in the lost meanings
of these words. There are losses so deep, loves so—I can't say.

The heart maps itself with symbols so no one else can read it.

There are reflections on the water that are her own dreams.
There are moments when her shadows disguise themselves as first light.
Above us, the plane has already left where its engine sounds.

What we don't hear is, in the end, the silence between heartbeats.

There are losses so deep. Now the sky is weighted down
with memories. Losses so deep. Even our shadows desert us.
I see, then, whatever we know we know by its absence—lives
that once travelled the old roads now barely perceptible
depressions through the woods, the invisible particles we take
on faith because of the paths they leave on a laboratory screen,
the odor of bear or deer we cross on a trail, the lives that continue
between flashes of last night's fireflies.

> *What we don't touch*
touches us, which is why we turn back as if there were someone
there, which is why we turn back each time.

And this morning,
above us, invisible stars the daylight hides begin to map for us,
secretly, new paths our hearts had seemed to despair of,—those
vapor trails that linger longer than they are supposed to, the wake
of the boat that echoes perhaps endlessly, shore to shore,—if only
we can believe in them without ever seeing where they are.

Listening to the Band at Bar Prulcek,
in Ljubljana, Slovenia

Some secrets can't quit /memory fast enough
—William Matthews, "Bucket's Got a Hole in It"

"When I was alive," we say as Poceni Škafi (Broken Bucket)
strikes up *"When the Saints Go Marchin In,"* because it seems
we are living on one of those multi universes that float,
as the science says, simultaneously, like bubbles beyond
our own. So, for a while we can smuggle our own feelings into
whatever tune comes next. For a while, that is, we can just
forget the bombings in Manchester and Baghdad. For
a while we can seem to live on one of those alternate worlds.
So then it's "My Bucket's Got a Hole in It," their signature tune,
meaning the way our beer and memories escape so easily
but also the porous bucket as broken condom. At least
that's what the crowd yells, and maybe it is only in music
that our contradictory worlds really appear. Maybe
it really is the music of the spheres that holds us all
together. Maybe those swallows circling the outside patio
really are arranging themselves as notes arriving from
another age. So it seems it is also 25 years ago, another
side of town, listening to the bar's crackling speaker's voice
Louis Armstrong's relaxed phrasings on *Bucket* which seems
to hold the exploding world together just south of here.
Jack Teagarden's trombone sliding with Earl Hine's
trumpeting piano over each atrocity, not to blot them out
but to provide some hope. So it seems the day gives away
nothing it needs to keep being the day. So it seems for
the couples rising now to dance as the quartet's trumpet
calls them to the floor. Even those swallows around the
patio seem to be keeping time, though we know it can't
be kept. And now the band responds by shifting into Swing.
It is not enough to understand this life if you only live it once.

Like Cemetery Blues

I don't want no drummer. I set the tempo.
—Bessie Smith

It is possible nothing happened. It is possible
the dawn's red shawl draped over the hills is
not a warning. The early hummingbirds dart
about indecisively. Doubts collect on the rough
undersides of leaves. Even the mockingbird
can't settle on one voice. There were images
last night that struck like the momentary visions
revealed by bomb flashes. It's possible it was only
a nightmare. Flocks of memories fly off to
return unrecognized. Reality is undergoing
another rehearsal. That's why it is possible
to forget the albino children of Mozambique
sold for body parts. It is possible the boy
riding his bike through the minefield will
make it. "I'm going down to the cemetery
'cause the world is all wrong" sang Bessie Smith
in 1923, the same year *Popular Science* praised
the Eugenics program in Kansas. It was
Jimmy Jones's block chords marching steady
with her to the grave's edge. This morning
I am reading the poems of Tonci Marovic
who believed he'd turned into a sparrow
that visited him on the windowsill of his prison
cell in Split in 1991 a few months before
his soul flew off. These images are the lizards
darting into crevices in his stone walls.
It is possible that Bessie Smith knew about
the women being sterilized in Baltimore as
she sang, because all these images are connected.

This morning her voice is trying to make sense
of all this terror as it plays in the background.
What we know are points on a compass
that has no needle. It is possible either despair
or love, weeping or song will win out here.

The river here doesn't listen to what we say—
it has its own words for what hides beneath
the surface. Every death sticks in the throat.
In the years she sang the Black men of Tuskegee
were a control group treated for their syphilis.
They were told only that they had "bad blood."
The shadows we cast sometimes paint a picture
that has nothing to do with what we want to see.
Bessie tried to live inside the one perfect song
she never found. After the wreck, she lay for hours
by the side of a Mississippi road and never woke.
The owl's cry slept in the grass. I believe it was a tune
she knew. It was a dream of stars not yet born.

Do you think I am crazy dreaming all this?
It is the song we must continue to sing. "It's
a Long Old Road but I Know I'm Gonna Find
the End", she'd sing a few years before the end,
but she never meant where "The Devil's Gonna
Get You." This morning the road leads off like
a prophet. The river keeps its own time which has
nothing to do with what I hear her singing. There,
a mother duck looks back at the ducklings who are
following her like notes on a staff. Sometimes music
changes the color of the air, sometimes it questions
the very solidness of the earth we walk upon.
It is possible she sensed the magnolia blossoms
swaying above her as she lay waiting in the dark.
Above her the mockingbird had already adopted
her voice. For a moment the sky opened as a whole note.
For a moment it was all jay and robin and sparrow.
For a moment the earth responded as one block note.
This morning I think it is possible to believe anything.
It is possible we are all sparrows on a windowsill
waiting for the song that lifts us beyond ourselves
because *the world is all wrong*, and because we still believe.

Elegy: Reading Keats and Listening to Clifford Brown

Kari Harvey, 1982 – 2016

The moon is sleepwalking through the trees. A stupor
of fog slides drowsily over the channel's surface. Two herons
rise out of it with an enthusiasm of wings. Asteroid 2016103
has played a cosmic blues with us as it shadows our orbit,
now behind, now ahead of us. Some astronomers call it
Love. "What Is This Thing Called Love" Clifford Brown blew
at Basin Street, February 1956. In a few months his car would
tumble in eighth notes down an embankment. A few months
from his own death Keats would improvise a new ending
for Spenser's *Faerie Queene*, his last verse. He wanted,
he said, to carry the moon in his pocket. He, too, would bear
his secret like a hairline fracture of the heart. He's buried with
his love's unread letters. "Joy Spring," Clifford would write for his wife.

Here the leaves drip with dew, the cicadas improvise upon
each other's melodies. Trumpet flowers want to play to the clouds.
Sometimes the words for things sound louder than the things.
Too many of them seem to be crowding into this moment.
Brownie would manipulate chords so he wouldn't have to
stay in a single present. I think he knew how time frays into
other times. You have to live in "uncertainty and doubt,"
wrote Keats, you have to lose your identity in the music,
you have to "choose between despair and Energy," he added.

It was with that energy Clifford chose to attack each note
that seems now to breach like a dolphin. He'd race and swim
around his horn, Dizzie said. Is there a water beneath
the water, a sky behind the sky? A note between the notes
we don't hear? The moon is gradually wearing out. We don't
see those asteroids that burn up their secrets in the atmosphere
and, if we do, we name them shooting stars. No matter.
It was all blues and gospel at their ends." I'll Remember April,"
Brownie goes on. We all have too many postcard memories,
too many slips of paper we can no longer read. Every idea
disappears behind its word the way one landscape gives way
to another over millions of years. There's always a bigger picture.

How many lives like these flick out of the corners of our eyes
before we can describe them? It is our shadows that tell us what
or who has been missing. At night we know there are boats
on the water by their running lights. Even Moses couldn't describe
the backside of God. "Heard melodies are sweet, but those unheard
are sweeter," wrote Keats. Finally, now, the mockingbirds begin
their own improvisations. They can tell you everything about the past.
I have no idea why they choose which sound to riff off. There are
so many unused words I have pocketed out of sight, so many
things I should have said or done. So many. How often the world
seems to arrive too late, that single note that hangs unheard. The secret
of this poem is the name I choose not to voice, the imperceptible sound
of the trumpet valve, the distant hum of galaxy M4 we never hear,
the silent paths those Jesus bugs leave on the water. Beneath them a few
bubbles poke the surface as if to explore another world. Above them
spiders are prophets because they weave a future between branches
they can see. A heron drinks the reflection of a plane. It doesn't know
like Keats' Lamia, which world it should enter. The sky's membrane
pulses with unplayed notes. "I always made an awkward bow,"
wrote Keats at the end. *Choose Now* is how Brownie's session ends.

Floating

What is there left to say about this free floating I?
—Paul Ricoeur, *Oneself as Another*

As when the raccoons approached and walked by as if
we were not there, or when the sudden overcast
wiped away our shadows, or when we were reading
how the universe keeps expanding but leaves us behind,
we began to think of ourselves like those mirages
that waver off the desert floor, maybe the invisible
force that drives the tumbleweed and kicks up
dust devils though they have nothing to do with real
devils which is the point after all, wondering here
how real we are not to be noticed, if we have been
distorted like those fun house mirrors, or like the fish
who are never where we think because of the light's
refraction, fractioning us, because we have forgotten
whatever it is we thought we were, what seems now
to float across the yard like those dandelion seeds
themselves too early, not heeding the calendar, or us,
which brings us to the point here, the women separated
from their children at the border as if they were not
real, only blown weeds or mirages in someone's scope
becoming smaller and smaller as we all are, knowing this,
sitting here letting history blow us wherever, the whole
universe watching us shrink into our own distances.

Triptych

When you spin the globe
                and touch that country,
it begins then for the child,
                caught by chance
in a circular frame,
                a tondo of sorts not unlike
those in the village church,
                and unlike the windows
in the mosques, as he steps
                out from behind the pocked
wall of what remains of
                his house because it is dusk,
it is safe, and he can
                almost taste the time,
can almost sense the few
                shrewd stars waiting
to play their hand,
                waiting as they do
in the enormous
                loneliness of space that lies
beyond the broken
                spines of trees the child
runs past for it is time
                the game begins, not just
the football on the dust lot,
                but the one seen
through the scope,
                that is of the Zastava M48
with its 7.92X57 mm
                load, nestled as it is
on its tripod, delicate
                as the legs of a spider,
blackened so as to avoid
                reflecting any revealing light

there, on the mountain that is
                    more like the spine of this
camouflaged man nestled out of sight,
                    a long but not impossible
shot, like unraveling
                    a rope until it is
taut, but now there is no
                    need to range or adjust
for wind, a wind that
                    hardly whispers
its warnings, above
                    the scratching of the
ground birds or secrets of
                    the hawk, no need now
to pull the trigger because yes,
                    now the boy steps, without
looking, and knows
                    before he hears
the land mine's click crumbling
                    into its own distant echo
as the light crumbles
                    through the trees and he
himself now seems
                    to know he is not there,
not here, while the other
                    gently removes the scope,
rises, leaves, carries
                    the Zastava as you would
a child, for he knows,
                    no need to look now,
knows already how the boy
                    has become smudged against
the sky, a kind of red scar
                    spreading mid-air,
and if you yourself looked
                    closely through the scope
known for its clumsy
                    design, the tonda
seems to quiver, and you
                    yourself can see now

the child's dreams shredded
              as he himself is
shredded, as the light is
              shredded, a prism effect,
a light-show swelling
              the air,—blossoming,—
a Calla lily on fire
              as—colorless—the other
children freeze even
              in this late hot sun,
afraid to step, wanting
              to be lifted out, angel,
helicopter, an epidemic
              of clocks turning too
fast, or broken, stuttering,
              yours, the heart's
aftershocks, love's aftershocks,

              *

              and those shocks that begin again
with your finger nudging
              the heart's tectonic plates
hidden beneath the continents
              on the globe in front of
you with its colorful spectrum
              of countries, the same
spectrum you gazed at
              in the school lab as the light
split itself apart through
              the pyramid prism and you
wondered how complex
              each simple thing could be,
and you pointed to where
              years later—(which is now
in time's twisted syntax),—
              you could hear hushed syllables
echoing unwanted meanings,
              but the child, low light
slashing through him, through
              a stand of live oak, reddish,

for the sun has begun
                to burrow into the hidden horizon,
as if the whole world were
                dying around him, the brush
decorated with thorns,
                stones that scar the land,
hears a rumor of something
                he doesn't yet understand,
shadows moving on their own,
                bird song without the birds,
roots sinking too deep
                to follow, and his own dreams,
there in the background
                like a swarm of yellow jackets
or the low hum of the interstate
                but, no, that is too distant
to hear,—the world now
                becoming less believable,
the backbone of the ridgeline
                wanting to turn into darkness
itself, there, where another man
                watches, remembering a
tortured light, a dozen
                headlights creating a stage,
a medieval play, a game,
                back then, masked, hooded,
the bonfire tossing light
                against the live oak trees
that still grab the air
                with their careless branches,
as they grabbed, carelessly,
                those lives he still doesn't know,
but where the child now
                hesitates, watches, yes, as if
looking at an earthen tondo—if
                he knew the name,—painted by
hate, like looking through
                those kaleidoscope tubes
you did as a child yourself
                amazed, but here you are

looking into the past
                that swirls dizzily,
a catacomb of ghosts,
                a honeycomb of knifed
ideas, leprous light,
                for back then darkness covered
the darkness, but now
                this tortured silence of
a rotten rope slung over
                a rotten branch, an image
from a story that had been
                only a story, a dream
that hangs there, empty,
                imagined, but also visible
as the sides hanging
                in the butcher shop or
the deer strung up for
                cleaning, still wondering
how it came here, or as
                the white laundry sheets gesturing
from backyard clothes lines
                like signal flags revealing how
once they could have been
                hoods, so, yes, he knows
that, and so knows better
                than the other, knows why
the hands of the town
                clock point always away
from the moment, accuse time
                itself of forgetting, like posters
thinking always of the future,
                not drilling into the past
as he is now, memories
                stuttering, crumbling
in his hands, wonders
                when he will stop living
those undreamt dreams

*

         or it begins again, the silhouette
against the blinds where
         the light fingers the globe
to where the sound oozes
         through, more than sound,—
a window, movie screen,
         gallery frames of crucifixions,
a threat, what you dream
         alone in the woods at night,
moon wrapped in gauze,
         the trail melted away long ago,
so the child in this case
         hesitates now, his soul looking
desperately around
         to be somewhere else,
drops the flowers, more
         weed than flower, the way
Adam did at Eve's approach,
         that loss of innocence,
a loneliness like a single
         bell rope in the abandoned
clock tower of the church,
         its steeple pointing towards
the emptiness of space
         the child fills with imagination,
the heart blindfolded,
         a children's story, but now no longer
at the helm, now being the wrong
         knight, unhorsed, the wrong
maiden won, all these
         stories once read to him
in a cotton light, lost now,
         those days of games before
the man's terrifying arrival
         that circles him like starlings
as he passes the collapsed
         stone wall, the car up on blocks,
and sees the woman's face
         a jigsaw puzzle of scars,

the man's shadow
                    flailing in the blinds,
the music a loud glove
                    pressed over her mouth,
the child knowing who is
                    next, but hesitating
this one time, dreaming
                    a sky all his own, a door
only he can open, a path
                    quickly covered behind him
with time's leaves because
                    there are no words for this,
just his feelings uncoiling
                    among the faintest stars, a kite
cut loose, a hawk floating
                    as if on some invisible lake,
because it is about what is
                    missing, what the stream
running over the cliff
                    wants to fill, dusk
like a puddle filling
                    the valley, the catbird
raiding anyone's nest,
                    bats returning to the cave,
water filling the eye's
                    ducts, because he hesitates, yes,
to leave her here, the air
                    made suddenly of stone, night
snaking towards him
                    through the trees,—the threat, the door,
the sky, the loneliness,—
                    and so what do you tell him, what
do you tell any of them,
                    for it is you, no, we who have scoped
this out here, shadowed
                    their shadows, wandered among
their dreams, as if
                    they were not our own,
as if the mockingbird
                    did not imitate this voice

we ourselves invent, singing,
                    from his hidden branch as if
the dust of our lives did not
                    fall into the eyes of the dead,
as if our own soul might
                    finally pass through the tiny
tondo of a needle's eye,
                    though it may be that it cannot help
bringing night with it,
                    bringing these words falling into
themselves, standing as we are,
                    here, at dusk's boundary line.

String Theory

For Iztok Osojnik

In my dream of it nothing is
        where it should be. The puzzle of the horizon
            shatters. We gather the pieces.
Wood moths try to fill the spaces between
        branches. The bulbs we planted
            have already broken through.
Is this a dream or a memory? The wind stretches
        itself into a thin string that wraps itself
            around these words. Clouds
wrinkle like crepe paper. No, this must be a memory.
        A swing saying *yes* then *no* from
        the bomb's concussion.
What bomb? There were too many to count, too
        many places it fell. Its own words
            not yet invented. These dreams
sleep like palimpsests in ancient manuscripts.
        Not even the monks deciphered them.
            Did I say dreams? Is this the past
or the future? Moles keep burrowing their ancient
        questions in the yard outside. All right,
            then, this is now. Riding over
the potholes of memory The beginning never ends.
        The end is sealed. We put the best face
            on it, invent a new mask of words.
Climbers know, only the crampons hide the secret
        of the rock face. The world is everything
            that is the world, one philosopher
says. The universe is a hologram we keep copying from
        one generation to the next, another says.
            We don't see what it is we are.
In a few millennia the sun will sift its ashes through
        whatever is left of wherever we were.
            The moon will shatter like one of

those Sweetgum pods. That is no dream. It is
a memory pasted in the heart's scrapbook.
Hartley thought our dreams were
the heart's garbage dump. There are two owls outside
taunting each other which is neither dream
nor memory. It is now, when far from
here someone has driven a car into a crowd to say
something he doesn't understand. *You have
to learn to love him if you hope to
ever stop the death of your own heart,* someone prayed
later from the crowd. And so it is, only now
do I begin to see how all this is
connected. The past is always something just pending.
Every moment strays into another history.
In this way, too, the heart echoes
its own forgotten stories, as this evening, what prompted
all this—the fading, high pitched scream of
the rabbit some coyote had carried away,
the sound knifing its way through these memories,
through the tendons of lost words that showed
a way to love, finally, this flawed world.

Five Elegies

Traces
Remembering Tomas Tranströmer

Not like Zecheriah who became mute because he didn't
believe the angel's words. But instead, those few dates
traced in the table dust at the outdoor café, birthdates,
it turned out, for friends we might have in common. A few
years after the stroke. How does anyone not feel shuttered
at that? The sky was a mirror for what we never said.
Our words exist only for what is absent. Our loves exist
because the moonlight evaporates before we can hold it.
Sunlight splintered on the clouds. Our own reflections,
traced on the surface, continued downstream somewhere.
The roads, too, never agree on any destination. So it seemed
the moment we were waiting for got mislaid. It arrives now,
too late, as I am listening to your left hand piano that flutters,
a hummingbird questioning a flower, threading through
the heart with the silent language that angel would understand.

The Mudpuddle
Remembering Aleš Debeljak

It exists only in the mudpuddle just as Escher saw
another world at the bottom of his painting,
but here now, 8,000 miles from you, where
the moon tries desperately to reflect its reasons,
where the cat comes to sip and turns away,
where the tracks leading away disappear after
a few steps, where the sun now seems to only
paint shadows of tree limbs, and a few
passers-by who avoid the puddle, as it slips
down behind a hill, but not your shadow
which has wandered off without you into
its own darkness from the Peracica Viaduckt
where rope jumpers used to free fall into another
world, as above them the paragliders turned pages
of the wind writing new stories with each turn,

and beneath it all the tiny stream still cuts into
the rock on its desperate journey that knows no end.

Fog Rises from the Leaves
Remembering Tomaz Šalamun

Through the barren tree limbs and the fog
that lingers like a half-remembered thought,
the moon is a bright smudge that hides
whatever stars were around it. But nothing is
ever where or when we see it. I remember
the flashlights fingering their way through
ground fog as we searched for Ludwig.
Lipica. When was that? Leaves are scattered
on the ground like unused words.
Gravitational waves bend the light, and time.
Maybe that is why the child asked today,
when we lose time can we find it later?
Tonight it is almost two years.
Galaxies continue to flow in currents
and swirl in eddies like pools of water
the child was playing in.
There's a face in every word we remember.
That's why your own words echo here tonight.
Megla se dviga iz listja. Fog rises from the leaves.
Utrujen sem biti sam. I am tired of being alone.
Every word has a future tense the way Zechariah's
horses and trees stood for future worlds he couldn't see.
Today we are still trying to map the cosmos
though its pages are smeared with theories.
And who are we but metaphors for what we want to be?

Dawn on Amelia Island
Remembering Mark Strand

You can see through the sea oats, swaying as if
to escape or embrace the offshore breeze,
the freighter laden with stories we will never read.

Beyond the horizon *Dark Harbors* have begun
to appear. A few charcoaled branches still try
to capture the night from someone's cold fire pit.
A hermit crab scuttles looking for a shell to claim
as its own. The early fishermen are casting
for sand sharks. The breakwater doesn't fool
the tides. The history here seems eaten by
sea worms. It was here that the slaves died
of cancers from harvesting the indigo plants
for a few bright colors of cloth beyond
that horizon. The ships that carried their human
cargo have long ago sunk. *A few clouds bleed,*
you wrote. We only want *not to be left behind.*
And now, the morning light seems to explode
out of a live oak. Time is a verb with no subject.
Like the cosmic rays that pass through us every
minute. In the meantime the earth rotates a few
miles, and inches further along in its orbit,
leaving behind so few of our words.

Spooky Action at a Distance: an Elegy
Remembering Franz Wright

That woman, olive army jacket loose over her Salvation Army
skirt, has coaxed her shopping cart towards whatever life
the morning might bring. A few blackbirds are still trying
to deny the dawn. A dragonfly stops mid-air to imagine
a life beyond this one, then darts away as if to forget it.
Isn't that bee trying to sip from the soda can a bit pretentious?
The woman's dreams are bottomless. How does the woodpecker
know where to strike next? How does one distant atom know
what the other is doing? How does the wind that has come
such a long way know which windows to rattle? The stars have
already dissolved. Our dreams are locked under eyelids.
The distant mountains appear like hedges. The pale moon is
humbled. Birds celebrate the fact of air. Franz would know that
God sits around the fire under the overpass with the other migrant
workers. Their souls are made of blood. Anything that's anything
seems out of reach. If only he could supply their papers. If only

the day delivered on its promises. Eternity's mirror reflects us all.
It doesn't matter that the skywriter's message is already tattered.
A truck jackknifes. A train totters off the tracks. The woman knows
more than we do about pilgrimage. The workers know which
prayers are real and which aren't. The long narrow streaks of cloud
stretch towards the horizon as if some giant hand had reached
up from the earth and scratched the sky trying to get out.

Behind the Eight Ball

It's the way the six ball glances off the four and finds
its way to the side pocket is how Brother Linus explained it
in 1960, meaning how the halfback hits the hole then bounces
outside. Or it's the way one atom hits another and causes
a chain reaction was what the Brother we called "Red"
tried to tell us a few years later, explaining how this led
finally to Hiroshima's melting. Everything we know is just
a metaphor, Meister Eckhart wrote in 1303.

                                    Which is why
we can say the green felt surface of the table is like
the surface of a pond, and that we just sail from one rack
to another. Every metaphor controls us unawares.
A *dead shot* we say, not thinking what that could mean.
Or what we mean when we say how some militia runs
the table on a village.
                      It's when we believe our metaphors
that we are in trouble, turning them into facts like the way
John Wier in 1564 calculated confidently that there were
7 Million, 409 thousand, 127 demons working for Lucifer
under the middle management of 79 demon princes leading
to lots of bodies left smoldering at stakes or hung on wheels.
Or how the skull was thought, in Neolithic times, to be
the sacred source of the soul, which explains why they were
staked on castle walls so the victors could trap their spirits
and which led later to the guillotine. Every metaphor has
a history we hardly understand.
                      How did we get here?—
Of course: the chain reaction metaphor, bank shots, miscues,
the way we are always behind the eight ball of one
fanatic or another—some madman in Syria or warlord
in Africa, maybe a disgruntled employee with a gun and an idea.
This is when the surface of our lake rebels against its depths,
shivers for the lost stories flooded like towns beneath it.

You have
to play the angles, trace the trajectory off the diamonds
several collisions ahead to leave the cue where you'll be
set up to finish. There's no playing safe. Tonight a few reflected
meteors scratch the fabric of the lake's surface. You think
that's just an embellishment to fill the space? Every metaphor
refers to something we can't say. The blue chalk clings
to your fingers like history. We'd like to think it's only just
a game, and then, before you know it, it's your turn to break.

Apricot Pits: A Story

For Metka Krašovec

How often something seems to open the gate of the mind
and introduce itself when you expected another visitor.
Like the image of that gardener lining up apricot pits
on the casement of his wall, and offering me the fruit
over the garden gate—but I had wanted to start with
another scene, the fortified church at Hrastovlje, Slovenia,
just up the hill from us, a refuge from Turkish raids
centuries ago. We were standing there where two worlds,
two tectonic plates were colliding beneath us, one slipping
under the other imperceptibly except for occasional
earthquakes now and then, but that is not the story here.
I wanted to write how I came for the frescoes, long hidden,
"The Dance of Death," peasant to Bishop lined up on a wall
for their interview with Death, and how I came for a prayer.
Above them, creation frescoes on the ceiling seemed to linger
beyond their seven days as if to delay what the pilgrims
were headed for. A year earlier I lost a daughter and now
I feared a dear friend had started her own long dance
in a hospital not far from there with yet another treatment.
The day's heat revealed itself as a haze on the far cliffs.
The meadow grass was already browned. I remembered
then how apricot pits contain Laetrile, a kind of
last judgment treatment for cancer, and a poison,
which is why the gardener was removing the pits and
chasing the squirrels from eating them. "Zivljenje,"
        he had said, or "prihaja v življenje," Life, or coming into life,
what the church was trying to teach but what the gardener
seemed to teach so much better. Each apricot seemed to
shine like its own sun and world, like the many worlds
science says we inhabit, or will inhabit after all is done.
What could I tell my friend except how I walked around
the fortress walls to a path leading nowhere but where
it leads, which is where you want it to lead, beyond
the world you think you know, a world whose deadly
pits are seeds that bring forth new trees, new life,
"Zivljenje," to everything we thought would disappear.

TRAVERSINGS

(2016)

Hidden Paths

The Red Clay Cherokee here believe that the only true doors
lead to the Spirit World. Tonight, the moon behind the scattered
clouds leaves torn edges appearing like scraps of burning
parchment. These are the sacred transcripts of Spirits who
change their names for each watcher. It was near here that
Turtle rose from mud to carry the world on its back. Tonight I am
facing west which they say is the dividing line between death
and life. There are scars that look like clouds all over the sky
there. This afternoon a stray dog crossed before me so gaunt
and scarred it must have been looking for the western door.
In truth, every direction is a path towards love, towards
whatever is sacred, whatever calls from your soul. The first
people here believed they had been called up from that mud
by the moonlight songs of cicadas. It is the same song lovers use
to call us from our dead words. Today the windows were filled
with lady bugs, and a few curious hornets trying to find a path
to the sun. The wind sent the leaves up like bats. But tonight's
moonlight has sent the insects into their home in the woodwork.
If you want to rise again from the earth you have to let the moonlight
fall all over you the way some tribes believe that, at the end,
you have to scatter the ashes of the dead over fields of grain so that
beneath the harvest moon the dead will enter their food and live
with them forever. You have to love the earth you are part of.

Shuffled Memories

The sun is in a hurry to hide away as dusk scrambles through
the ridgetop pines. It is a discreet moon that reveals only what
it wants. You breathe out a little bit of your soul, someone said,
until there's nothing left. "They Can't Take that Away from Me"
Lester Young's clarinet played plaintively, but they can. When
your dreams die, what's left? Tonight the stars seem bankrupt.
It's getting darker. The roots had already taken hold when they
found the mass graves in Mexico. Someone is shelling someone
else they can't see, will never hear. The windows just give back
our own images. So here's Lester again making his clear blues
from our shuffled memories. But so much stays hidden—the life
of that thirteen-thousand-year-old girl found in a Yucatan cave,
all those histories hidden away in Paleolithic burial mounds or
submerged under flooded shorelines, what can they tell us? Maybe
it is our own secrets that define us. The owl won't reveal his own
position. The moles have their own world. The mockingbird is
trying to correct all this from its hidden nest in the Mulberry outside
the window. The darkness is a shawl that seems to comfort him.
They can't take that away from me Lester keeps playing though
his own hidden memories would burst open some years later.
Maybe the dark side of the moon, or the hidden fault lines, or
the silences inside his notes, would say all we need to know. But
now the fading moon slips behind a new cloud. The roots keep
growing. The shells keep falling. The darkness seems to mean
more than it is. So Lester plays the lyrics, their invisible words
that haunt our dreams, because in the end, it is reality that has to
imitate our art, as Lester knew, *No they can't take that away.*

Sea Changes

How deep is the ocean is what Tommy Flanagan played, 1996,
a kind of poet, as if he were a ray gliding elegantly into the depths.
How high is the sky is what the man on the stone park bench
under a sputtering streetlight said as he argued with the clouds.
In medieval times they thought the sky was surrounded by ocean.
A sparrow pauses on my windowsill, listens to the disc, flies off.
They are clanging together rail cars to make a train to someplace
further than we'll know. The moon pulls us invisibly as it does
the tides. Except for our music we are all just blanks in someone's
memory. After a while we too forget about the girls taken in Nigeria,
the men beheaded or burnt alive. What is the color of silence?
You can hear Flanagan's silence while Peter Washington surfs
around on the bass. The girls' village was cold coals and body parts.
Already the trees have forgotten their leaves. The wind gusts are
playing to each other. A mast of light seems to rise up into a space
between the clouds. Part of us remembers more than we know.
There are answers we never hear, drowned in our deepest dreams.
The refugees at the Aid Station were waiting for names they hoped
they'd never have to hear. I don't think that sparrow will return.
But you can still hear his music, a few careful notes and then a trill.
Sound travels further in the depths of the ocean than here, but goes
nowhere in space. And so we play on, hoping to be heard. And you,
you'd hope, like Flanagan, you could play through your scuttled heart.

Evensong

How does it do that, the wind, read the desire of flowers?
I swear their fragrance was the color of sunset. I am watching
the scuffed sky turn dark and remembering too many friends
who followed it into the echoes of their own words. This early
in Spring a mold has begun to betray the dogwoods. I once
believed that silence revealed something of eternity. I once
believed in the geology of the soul. Today I was astonished
at how the new redbud leaves take the shape of tiny hearts.
Even a few hummingbirds have mistaken them for flowers.
Does the night blooming cereus on my windowsill believe
it is not a cactus? Not far from here the clear-cut forest has
nothing left to believe in. There is no myth we have that is
not blind to that. The birds there have no idea that we exist.
It is not enough to claim some Adam dropping his bouquet
at Eve's darkening approach. He notices a chipmunk settling
on a stump. A few fish come to the surface as if to test the air.
A mockingbird opens the petals of its wings to attract a mate
with a flash of white against the gathering dark. The heron
who has been hiding all this time slaps the air awake as if
to remind us how happy we are to be here, now, accepting what
the wind brings, and loving the unbelievable fragrance of sunsets.

What It Is

It is that phosphor light skating out from under the low
swamp fog. It is the hearth's glow long after the house has
collapsed in on itself. It is the space the coffin makes
in the earth. No, the memories climbing to the surface
along the roots of flowers. The man reaching into his heart
to see if it has its own reasons. It's the way we put the past
on the rack to extract secrets about the future. It's not
the distance out there but in here. It's whatever has made
our dreams wander off the trail we had hoped to follow.
Clusters of dust wander through space hoping to collect
into planets. It is the breath we want so dearly to keep
but must give up. It is my friend saying *enough* and it's
my leaving a stone at his grave when I visit. It is everyone
I haven't told, everyone I embrace so secretly, every word
that remained caught on the spindle afraid for the love
it might weave. It is the only way you can let the sky
lean down to touch you, the only way the sweet terror
of love means anything. Each shadow hides its own
peculiar light. The river near here once ran backwards
trying to revise its own dream after a quake. It's why,
still, the ripples in every river point against their currents.
Even the heart beats against itself. It is the waterfall
blinking its light through the pines, and the pines nodding.
It is for this the heart's magma erupts again and again.

Not Here

The moon only rehearses what the day has taught it.
The last rooks map again the wind's currents. Time is
measured here by the loudening voices of tree frogs.
Earlier, the bear and I stood across the ravine exchanging
shadows the way lovers do in those medieval romances.
Neither of us cared that a planet thirty-three light years away
shed its atmosphere in a trail of gasses nine million miles long,
nor worried when that would happen here. What we were
waiting for was the annual June show of fireflies who
synchronize themselves into trailing ribbons of light
undulating back and forth through the woods. It is a way
of saying we are here, we are one, a romance of light. Through
the lattice work of branches we watched another universe
take shape. Beyond, the skeletons of a failed village were
becoming its own forest. Now and then a coyote claimed
its own space. A few shy stars seemed humbled by it all.
A few bats seemed confused by echoes from what they
must have thought was a flying snake. Hypnotized maybe.
Was it a coincidence we met there, two beings from different
worlds amazed at how those undulations guided the beating of
our one heart? He turned away then as reverently as from
an altar. For a moment the earth tottered on its axis. I don't think
you can love the world any more than this, each of our breaths
trailing off into a night that will never know we were here.

OUT OF PLACE

(2014)

About This Poem

*At the beginning. . .which is to awaken you to the right kind of Joy
in serious times, we must list all those who have been killed
since I last wrote. . . .*
—Bonhoeffer, 1942, Germany

It has to account for its untied shoelaces as well as its Extermination
Camps. Sitting among all those languages in the Munich beer garden.
Hitler's first speech a few blocks away. A masked ball where
the costumes are all switched around. Those carnival grab bags
filled with joy or remorse. Above me the clouds are paralyzed.
I have to wipe the dust from my soul. The wind holds its breath.
Bosnia, 1994: one group of men forced to bite off the testicles
of another group. Others to stand in the snow till their feet rot.
These things orbit now like a planet too far to see. Even the bee
can't figure a way out of my stein. Light staggers through the trees.
Every moment is filled with other moments. According to Bell's
Theorem whatever happens to this bee influences a history yet
to be written. Like the seed stars that smudge the trail of Mira as
it slips across the sky. All my maps are smudged with atrocities.
There are so many voices that are our own voices. Rhythm is just this
oscilloscope of the soul. We come from a place that has always
been inside us. Our words migrate helplessly. The world reflects
only itself. Which is why we have to create our own memories.
The paths from here spread out like cracks in ice. The man
across the table's from Krakow. He doesn't want to talk about
the occupation and its lives turned to smoke. Only the mechanical
Trumpeter in his church spire. The song stops where his real
ancestor was felled by an enemy's arrow. In the silence that follows
don't we all have to begin again? At the end of a line, the door
left open for a moment where you can fall in love, remember
what you wanted to forget, forget what you wanted to remember.
Why do we think our metaphors will save us? The world is only
itself. Time is just our way of imagining it. At least the bee has
ultraviolet vision to see everything we can't. We have to light
our dark spaces with the sputtering matches of our words.
We have to follow wherever they lead us. There's this little
hole in existence we all pass through. Someone is always entering.
He's the one who invents me while I think I am writing about him.

Sarsaparilla

For Phil Levine

I'll never know what words my Uncle Bernard chose
to connect the Belgian landscape with his B-17 as it
pancaked down after helping his crew bail out. "Sarsaparilla,"
my father says, because he and Bernard used it to mean
"surprise," and "there's nothing left to do," but that was 1954
and we were making Sasparilla, a kind of intense root beer,
to store it in those dark green used bottles in the closet.
I believed that if the wrong word seeped in the bottles
would explode. Bernard went down as Bonhoeffer was
looking for words to argue against Hitler. Spain was
already lost. I would learn later that it was not history
but space that mattered.

                                You can see dusk expand now
across the pond's surface. The wind gets tangled
in the trees. Words disappear into the woods, trails
into forgotten ravines. It's as if each word enclosed
a secret meaning impossible to guess, or the voices
we thought we buried still echoed like the bells
they used to place above graves in case the dead had
something to say.

                                I think that's what Hardy meant
when he had his corpses listen to gunnery practice
instead of the apocalypse. My father knew how all wars
just try to find another word for space. I remember him
telling the story of Joseph yelling from the bottom of a well
while his brothers claimed his land. Today a few
words crash through a Sinai border crossing,
a few others build a town on someone else's land,
another scatters its meanings across a temple
whose words it cannot understand.

                                    Here, a few
stars call out. A few late birds scour for crumbs.
There are languages no one understands. There are
three new stars from the Milky Way each year
that have no name. That's ten million since
our first ancestors walked on earth. Sarsaparilla!
my father would have whistled. I don't know
a better reason to keep looking for words that rise
beyond us like the red *sprites* that light the edge
of space and send their secret messages into
the furthest corners of the universe.

                                    Tonight
shapes start to speak from the pond's surface under
the borrowed light of the moon. When one of
my father's bottles burst the others echoed it
filling the room with the sweet smell of failure.

Joseph, from the bottom of a well, could see,
even at noon, day stars he had thought were invisible.
Sarsaparilla he too would have cried in hope if he knew
the word. There is one star which is the bottle galaxy,
edging towards a Black Hole, but spraying its words out,
as my father knew, with its countless and relentless stars
that mean the love that connects us over time which is
space, which is all the love we have, or could ever have.

Bosnian Elegy

The tops of trees still clutch, fiercely, the last light.
There's a bird caught in the chimney. Its complaint
trembles down the empty corridors of the heart.
The moon struggles to define itself behind a few thin
masks of cloud.
     I remember the Sax player in Sarajevo
playing *Solitude* as if Coleman Hawkins fingered
the keys as he did on that old recording my father
kept, each layer of harmony rubbing against the wall
and slipping through the alley to where, later, the market
would be bombed.
     Why can't I get that song out of my head?
How much space does any memory take up? After
a while our pasts become abandoned buildings, or like
the sudden supernova whose light appeared for a few days
before moving through space to another galaxy.
          There's
always another mass grave to discover. The crickets begin
to panic. For a while our memories fall into the crevices
of the mind. Our words imitate our losses.
        For a while
we too can forget the love we didn't show or the people
we have hurt.
    We become the empty spaces in our dreams.
Tonight, a few invisible stars still keep their distance.
I can hear the leaves fall through the darkness.
        In Hell,
Aeneas grabbed the empty air he thought was his mother.
Plato thought the real took up no space at all. All these
memories seem out of tune. Hawkins' solitude was all
that he could bear.
     In a while that chimney bird stops but sound
keeps coming. There's always an invisible wind that rips
at the stars. Sometimes I think there is an invisible *other*
who occupies every mirror.

My friend says she avoids
trouble by becoming invisible. My voice distrusts my ear.
There's always a few memories to scar the air. There's
no secret that is secret. Our hopes are only grace notes.

There's always that image I can't push aside, the family outside
Banja Luka, in the charred cellar, the man's fist raised above

the other bodies, melded in defiance where they were
burnt alive.
        Tonight the hissing of stars is more than I can bear.

Otherness

It is part of our disguise that our dreams are lived by someone else.
Thales dreamt an eclipse in 570 BC and stopped a war. You arrived
subconsciously in a sentence I was reading from a book I never
finished. What we say gets its meaning from what we don't say.
Persephone kept her love hidden underground. So much of what
we feel is habit. We need to search for a way to say what is real:
the air filled with the simple pungency of cut grass, the flowers
barely breathing, the black and azure butterflies mating in clusters
by the side of the trail, the melancholy taste of blackberries
some bear had abandoned at my approach, the stag that lifts
its head unconcerned, whatever drifts away, whatever stays.
How do we keep our own dreams from touching each other?
I remember, as a boy, fearing for the snail as is crawled out
from its shell, I imagined for love. I couldn't coax it back.
What we do is a metaphor for what we don't do. These are
the only ways to tell you what I mean. In Chagall's drawings
the faces of his lovers are surprised by their own sadness that
they have not become one of his angels smudged across the sky.
Their nights disguise themselves among the noontime shadows.
At the tomb, Mary Magdalene thought Jesus was a gardener.
What we know gets its meaning from what we don't know.
It is why we create stories for those Mayan cities still buried
beneath the jungles of Mexico. Everything is a metaphor.
Those butterflies on the trail, for instance, I thought
they carried part of the sky on their wings. Or the cloud
rising like a ruined column from some ancient site supporting
the sky's idea of it. In a while the wind convinces it to collapse
as it does with so many of our dreams. What we dream
gets is meaning from what we don't dream. Memory betrays us:
the sentence I read as you appeared was a piece of smooth
ocean glass where Nicholas of Cusa dreamt of spiritual beings
living near the sun. Anaximander knew we emerged from
sea creatures. What if you had appeared with those few snowy
egrets this morning who seemed puzzled or fearful at my presence?
What we love gets its meaning from what we don't love.

The air here seems filled with fragments of some other day.
In a drawing I saw once, my words shivered for how the stag
gazed tenderly at the wolves, as if to say they had no other choice,
as if to forgive them as they ate so ravenously from its side.
No, never again have I dreamt such a perfect love.

While You Were Away

Sleeves of sunset hung empty over the brown hills.
Ice from the North Pole kept floating this way. Locusts
sprouted like seedlings. I was floating under the ice
in my dream, but you never saw me. The windows were
boarded up. Later the clouds argued, then left in a huff.
There's a hidden tax in everything we say. I meant
for this poem to glow in the dark like one of those
old statues of saints. My father kept one on the dashboard
to guide the way.
                But aren't we always lost? Desire
punches a time clock that always reads the same hour.
There's a suspicion that today is really yesterday.
That crickets dream about being reincarnated as pure
sound. The bees wake as the sun hits the hive.
The sky is filled with late and clumsy birds.
Somebody's always ready to pickpocket the past.
There's a gap in the narrative the way a river
suddenly slips underground but flows on unnoticed.
Now they think the vegetative state has some neuron
activity. I worry that most of my own memories are
water soluble. There are places inside me so remote
the inhabitants never see each other. The worm never
sees the robin. White tipped reef sharks catch a prey
by sensing the electric impulses in its muscles. Auto
cannibalism occurs when the Hutu militia of east Congo
make their captives eat their own flesh. Feel free to add
whatever you want there, but it won't make it any better.

Every war is reincarnated as another war. Even Paul
retreated to a cave in the Tarsus foothills when things
went bad. He preached about love but nobody has
ever really withstood its test. Some of his flock never
returned. "A species stands beyond," wrote Dickinson.
Almost every species of small bird comes to my feeder.
Maybe everything is a test. Like how I am going to get you

back into this poem. "I'll git you in my dreams," Leadbelly
sang to Irene. This was going to be a Valentine poem
because today is Valentine's Day, which replaced Lupercalia,
the Roman fertility feast, but that was before the daily news
broke in. And before tomorrow had already forgotten us.

The great love poet, Leopardi, never knew a woman.
Modigliani loved every woman he met, and painted them
in order to leave them. Queen Nefertiti's eye make-up
stopped infections, but its lead base drove her mad.
She wanted to be born again as the brightest star. She read
her future in the cloudy hatchery of the Milky Way.
If space weren't a vacuum we couldn't bear its decibel level.
The Hutu slaughter women who learn to read, and joke that
it's a form of reincarnation. They think they live on
the dark side of the moon. The sky is gnarled with clouds.
There's a low fog covering another war in the foothills.
The stars are no longer the gods we took them for.
The moon is a turtle that needs to right itself.

I don't really know how to tell you all this. It's as if
I were left at the doorway of one of your dreams.
If only these words wouldn't conspire against me.
But even Love is an unsolvable equation. Leadbelly
kept singing because his own song never worked except
in his dreams. I'm still floating in mine. I don't have
any Faith in a solution. You can't just turn off the news.
It's getting late—best to guess *None of the Above*.
All we have left is the astronomy of Hope. The hills have
their own geometry. Paul said we devour our own souls.
Maybe it's just the way the day grows up and leaves us.

It all comes down to the same thing in the end which is
what everything has been pointing to since the beginning.
When you're gone, you see, all these worries spin around
like those childhood tops that zig zag until they bump
into something that stops them, like this, for example,
another simple mention of you, spinning endlessly on.

Signs and Wonders

The morning avoids us. The streets walk through town and
never look back. Trees whisper secrets and we think it is
just the wind. The echo of the moon is fading. There's a worn
saxophone in the corner filled with unplayed notes. The pigeons
on the walk nod their heads and mumble to its music. The water
a cactus holds is the desert music Williams so loved. The foreign
planet that has wandered into our own galaxy, origin unknown,
has a plan for us it won't reveal. And why should it? The soot
we leave on Tibetan glaciers melts them. Diseases creep
towards the warmer north. Someone invades a home or
a country and it hardly wakes an image. A child is torn by
an abuser and no one reports it. The man selling pretzels,
the man sleeping under the cardboard on the bench,
each one has his own shoebox of memories. Our own shoes
are filling with borders. The bonfires of our souls fall in on
themselves. It's as if we must tune our silences to a lost key.

Love? How do we give ourselves to another and not lose
our selves? We have to learn how even the objects around us
hide their pain. We can't listen to the heart's ventriloquists.
It's a fact that music raises our endorphin levels which kills pain.
Ben Webster, in "The Wee Small Hours of The Morning" would
let his tremulous breath slide emotionally beneath his
saxophone's sensuous fingering, but was called *Brute* for the pain
he'd inflict, later, in a bar. My father, listening to Gene Krupa's
wild drum, would say the emptiness behind each note is just
the ghost of what we could do to each other. How lucky we are,
he'd say, not to calculate the decay of our own sun. The light hides
now behind skirts of rain. When scientists let hydrogen antimatter
collide with matter we delight in its pure energy and try
to ignore the destruction that always follows. These are all
the signs I know. They point to a world behind this one. Webster's
bulging eyes would tell us there is always more. The tracks of
the past out distance our dreams of it. And what was he gesturing
towards, years later, my father, his mind nearly porous, seeing those
three frightened pigeons, if not the pure, inescapable flight of his heart?

Visionary

I could feel a few dying stars hovering over my shoulder
but that wasn't it. Not the fact that there are so few
sunspots anymore, and therefore fewer Northern Lights.
Not the problem of the thinning Arctic ice. And yet weren't they
all connected somehow? Weren't they symptoms of something
I couldn't see. How many people saw the Naked man fleeing
Christ's betrayal in Gethsemene? Fish nibble at the moon's
reflection. Camels have two eyelids, one transparent,
so they can see in sandstorms. We see only what we want
to see, only a fraction of what this stone has seen in a few
billion years. Now the stone wants to be an apple. The night
splinters. The sky trembles piteously. The real world appears
in the reflection of the soldier's face on a green radar screen.

Maybe there are some things we are not supposed to see.
The town beneath the lake. The cells that will divide mercilessly
in a few decades. I have been looking at Chagall for whom
every object is transparent. He thought that some of his dreams
were dreamt in other people's minds. That's why his images
echo each other from distant points on the canvas. Everything
we see hides a world someone else sees. If you don't finish this
poem it won't exist. Neither will I. Where do we come from when
we come to ourselves? There's a common thread that hasn't
been established yet. Cendrars said that Chagall painted a church
with a church, a cow with a cow. He painted his own love, Bella,
floating up to kiss him. A hawk's flight unravels the thread we never
knew was there. There's a smell of smoke smudging through
the trees, but no fire.

These words migrate towards invisible
meanings. It would be hard to predict what follows.
Each hour seems ready to kidnap the next for ransom.
How many orphans blindly follow some warlord around
the streets of Mogadishu with an AK-47 and sack of grenades?
This is not the symbol or allegory you might take it for.

127

Behind them, if you look carefully, there's a mother fleeing
her burning house with a wheel barrow full of children.
She seems to gaze from the beginning of time. The day turns
into ash. The evening is exhausted. It lies like a shed snakeskin.

It is only slowly now that the poem gathers itself around
these unexpected events. In Chagall's "Poet Reclining,"
the pastoral world behind him is both dreamt and real.
He seems to lie in front of, not in the picture. You can't see
who is in the building or in the woods. You have to look for
what is out of place. We need, like Blake, to look "through
and not with the eye." The paths from here spread out like
cracks in ice. The skaters trace patterns you can only see
from above. How am I going to see my way clear of all this?
Everything I say brings its endless army of associations.
In another poem the woman would be pushing a shopping cart.
We can hope for another scene to emerge out of the shadows.
There's nothing we can do about the guns or the warlords.
It will have to show a way that looks like truth, but
it will have to show it through these broken windows.
You have to see it to believe it, but you'll never see it coming.

What Comes Next

There is nothing more deceptive than an obvious fact.
  —Arthur Conan Doyle, "The Boscombe Valley Mystery"

There are knots of time so tangled they frighten me.
There are bodies turning into tree ornaments in Mexico.
There is the mother driving her kids into the lake
in Illinois. The antibiotics in our meat will finally kill us.
There are mornings that trudge out of the darkness
we made for them, and into the darkness we make for them.
What keeps him playing, the homeless man with his guitar
missing the bass string? He's playing *Believe it, Beloved,*
the way I remember Django Reinhardt on those scratchy
CD's. Someone drops him a coin. A robin in a dying tree
tries to answer. Sirens rake the sides of buildings.
The air has no air to breathe, the sea has no sea to define it.
There are knots of time. There are mornings. The roots
of clouds sway uncontrollably. Dreams rise up through
The chimneys. How difficult it is to write to you now.
There are shadows that deny the light that made them.
There are palms lined with regrets, hearts spotted with mold.
What am I supposed to say about the latest massacre
in Nigeria? Or the killer of a couple over a custody fight?
There are knots of time so hurtful. *Time on My Hands*
Django played so serenely he could believe in angels
gliding up and down the neck of his guitar in a melancholy
tango. In the meantime there are coffins taking the place
of forests. There's another makeshift shrine to a fallen
policeman. Are you just going to let me go on like this?
These truths appear and disappear like aging planets.
When we breathe we take in air from the farthest places
and return it to worlds that have yet to appear. Why
has it become so difficult, then, to believe in the invisible?
You might say that all of this has nothing to do with you,
or that it is simply that we are lucky to be alive, as lucky
as Reinhardt who burnt himself on his own artificial
flowers, crippling two fingers yet still went on in time
playing sudden tremolos behind Bill Coleman on *Sweet Sue*
in 1937. Which brings me back to all that fear, and so much

more we never see, but also how much meaning we never
guess is in a dot we thought was a star, but turns out to be
a galaxy of millions of stars, planets with their own secrets,
or the simple way a homeless man struggles with his own
story, waiting like all of us, for what comes next, the way
a salmon climbs a waterfall towards what it cannot see but loves.

Letter from Slovenia

For my granddaughter, Anna Marie Thomson

I once stepped into the same river twice.
That was when I had a constellation stuck
in my throat. You were waiting on one of those
stars to be born. Today a bee's wing creates
enough wind to drench the planets. The moon
begins to untangle the shadows which
the mountain tries to tie to its cliffs. Each beat
of your heart shakes a few other stars awake.
I hope you never have to know the horrors
that cover the newspaper I am trying to write
over. Even the river pauses to listen to its own
reflections. All the children are Angels, the taxi driver
said in Baltimore last month quoting the Koran,
but in the first few weeks we all look
like the same kidney bean. I can see you
chasing butterflies and pigeons the way
your mother did. This is how my skin can hold
the memory of your touch though you should not
arrive for another week now which is exactly when
the sky will have to borrow another color
if it wants to still be the sky. You will know
your own mother as the sound of running water,
your father as the fallen petals that show
which way the water flows. When I touched
the statue of Madonna dell'Orto in Venice
for you the other day, a white chalk stuck to my hands
and I held my own clouds to the sky. What holds
the clouds up so effortlessly? Now the moss
breaks loose from the river's stones. Clouds drift
away from their roots. The river thinks
it can run uphill. Someday, when there are
only my words for you, you will hear them
as the timpani of stars. Today a hawk
flew next to the car before darting out
across the fields. I thought it was you. Each
word, each gesture, is a feather for our wings. Later,
I ran down that mountain and landed in your name.

Letter from Tuscany

For my granddaughter, Emily Frances Thomson

Inside you, a dream has begun to ignite the stems
of flowers. Now that you have arrived, this Tuscan
sky seems full of seeds. Where you are, I watched,
with your sister, a shadow that seemed to promise your shape.
The tree above me is tattooed with swallows. A few
dart around this table. I think they are memories
from your future. I think the train in the valley below is
searching, like me, to find a world that doesn't
exist yet. By then, there will be no need
to worry about the wars and tortures, the drizzle
in our hearts from this tangle of hours you'll hear about
later on. Now, even the rocky light holds
the hills in its hands. The clouds are stroking
their bald crests. I can almost slip my own arms
into the sleeves of the wind—it smudges the slender
olive leaves. Now the dark is folding the hills up
for the night. I am this happy: my pockets full of
butterflies, each breath setting off on its own
road. There's a distant smoke waiting for its fire.
The whistle is waiting somewhere for the train. I will
have to learn the language of roots. The moon's
flour covering the trees. Your words for mother,
Father, sister, light, swallow, love.
The life you have before you have a life.

Negative Capability

*. . .the ability to live in uncertainty and doubt without
any irritable reaching after fact or reason.*
                                        —Keats

Some days I don't know how to live. This is not about that.
It doesn't matter that there are a few snarled thunderstorms
to the south, a few nails of light hammering the hills to the north.
I'm sitting on the impossibly spherical space of a Reiman
universe where straight lines are curved, where nothing ever
ends or begins, and amid the invisible village of Lidice razed
by the Nazis, everyone killed or deported, even the trees, even
the old graves uprooted. I'm sitting in a rose garden that is
no longer a street, where no longer the lamp post lights
a nameless man who once played his bandaged sax to the moon.

How do you measure what's lost when it's no longer there?
I imagine he plays *Round Midnight* though he couldn't
know it the way Sonny Rollins did in 1996, pausing, diving
deeper, floating across the surface then sinking to a kind of
moan. It's what I am listening to now, the sax trying to say
it has nothing to do with what happened here, apologizing.
In fact, this is not about anything until you say it is. We assume
a reader who understands, but there's nothing to understand
here. The sky hides the sky, stars hide other stars. But this is
not about any of that, because so much has been distorted
to make it sound like an easy truth. There's no way to defend
ourselves against these nightmares. Not today with a killer
shooting children at a Peace Camp in Norway, another shooting
into a skating rink in Dallas.
                            But this is not about any of that
either. Some roses have wilted, others start to bloom. Every
memorial tries to say what can't be said. Maybe I should listen
to the hidden bird on the side of one of these ghost trees.
I wish he would replace the clock. But today even our own
footprints seem outlawed. There are warehouses of emotion
we rarely touch, piles of newspapers with no front page,
mirrors refusing reflections. Sometimes our shadows shiver
without us. Sometimes tomorrow falls on yesterday. This is

not about the reefs of stars our hopes are dashed upon, not
our splintered skies, however true, though one story always
reflects another. I mean, this has nothing to do with memory,
which is never enough. Our lives are just a sideshow here.
This is not about the flight of crows passing through my soul.
There shouldn't be a way to say anything here that will last,
no way to start again. Every pier ends in failure. I think it has
something to do with the heads of the unborn that turn away.
Sometimes we call to them, and sometimes we see more
when we look through a spider's web. Why does a single tear
weigh more than the earth?

                     All our memories are rubble
no one can rebuild. I don't know what they sing, the angels
haunting these fields. And who could listen to Sonny Rollins
the way I do now among this orchestra of bullets still spitting
into the earth from another age. Sometimes we are amazed
just to find that we are still alive, as the whole world begins
to move in the light of a paused note, and I begin to write this,
the roses stammering, the group of 49 bronze girls and 42
bronze boys scanning the valley as if they entered our thoughts,
which is why they are still so worried, the levees of language
failing, the heart floundering, the world disappearing into an
endless tune that waits for the nothing we must always become.

Everything All at Once

There's a buck beyond the far end of the field
but he doesn't know he's dying, couldn't know,
that is, the patience behind the sights he's caught in.
The dignity of just being alive, the freedom of it.
So many sounds coming from the grass and the trees.
On the farm further past the woods a finger of smoke
desperate for a word to contain it. A few dilapidated
clouds. We have come here following a map from
memory. The horizon refuses to go on. You can feel
the sun as it flees. How is it we feel the need to lose
what we love? There's a star or a planet just starting
to shutter behind the leaves as if to deny the darkness.
You can hear the buck knock its knees together
then urinate on them, rubbing it in, to attract whatever
doe is nearby. He won't come into the field just yet.
How many times have we practiced our own deaths?
Our truths seem as packaged as these bales of hay.
A hundred and fifty years ago two armies slaughtered
themselves here. Maybe that is what the buck senses.
Far beyond that horizon a woman looks into the bomb
crater that was her home. It is the last word in
a sentence of many words. She could live on any map.
The early mapmakers created worlds that put them
at the center. One described the earth as a yolk
in an eggshell. Believe me, it is that delicate.
Aren't our first words for what we don't have
or have lost? Don't we want everything all at once?
The light's shredding. There's still time to fire.
What is there to feel but the way sometimes we seem
safe and something in our own voice surprises us
to see we cared more than we expected. The buck
hides inside his own meaning. The silence of the hawk
just overhead seems to stop time. Some words are
wounds that do more damage than a shot that rings out.

At The Confederate Graveyard, Chattanooga

The world is full of marvelous things that words could not keep.
—Marvin Bell

Starlight blows across the graves of the slaves whose stones
disappeared, or never were. Similarly, the song of some hidden bird
shivers as the light does on the inside of your eyelid. Just as I say
that I realize how easy our words carry us from one thing to another
before we understand what it means.

                                    I think how there are no nouns
in the natural world. And how often is that what we mean we never
say, but that what we say we often never mean.

Here the leaves seem
to turn into air. The clouds rewrite themselves as other clouds.
All evening I have been haunted to think of you as gone. Across
the path, the stones of Confederate soldiers become their own shadows.
One legend has it that souls wander outside their bodies only
to remember things they never saw. Maybe we are just stories
telling other stories. We think the dead live in us, but it is we who live
in them.

By now that bird is making impossible requests. It seems
to rise out of its own song. Above it, the Milky Way appears as
a huge scythe across the sky which is, I fear, the kind of sign
no one wants to understand. Maybe its stars are just another failure
of darkness. Still, in all that darkness, the Voyager probe is still
looking for the birthmark of the universe. How tragic that we never
speak the one word that gives meaning to what we will become.

Here, moonlight uncovers what is forgotten, but what we remember
stays hidden. It is as if even this mention of you didn't exist.
The horizon crumbles behind a few buildings. How many of those dark
corners of the sky are stars that have burnt out like the names of the lost.

How easy it is for a poem about death to become a poem about love.
How easy it is for our dreams to lie to us. I think that is why the song

of that bird tells us to speak like the wind, because our dreams must
sift through everything if we are to believe what they imagine for us.
I think this is why the Egyptians took out the brain but preserved the heart.

Or why the Brazilian Indians think of people as halves of one another.

What I love are the moments between notes of that marvelous bird.
This is the first thing I have to tell you: inside each of its notes my heart
beats. The empty branches tell us why there is something rather than
nothing.

      I know now what the man knew when he called this place
"savagely tender." He is sleeping at the far corner where the path ends
as if his story were beyond rescue. But I should tell you also that this
poem has been written over the erased drafts of an earlier poem
whose characters were only these headstones, the way that man
had etched a name above the faded dates of a distant relative.
And this too is a story we live inside when we no longer know
what to call it, a story whose words are the only truth we should
trust, for what is rescued dies, but what is lost lives forever.

Riptide

For my sister, Nancy

How many times have we reduced our lives to a wrinkled map?
How many places has a broken street sign or compass led us?
How many times do we believe the invisible—like the riptide
that ferries the empty skiff into the next state? This morning
everything is so still we can hear the tides turning inside us.
There are vapor trails already shredding the past above us.
An uneasy breeze tears the lazy fog from the sea surface.

What we were is never what we are. A few cormorants
disappear below the swells, then rise to shake off whatever
it is they have dreamt. We are already in heaven, wrote Tillich,
but we have to know where to look. How many times?
We blink almost 20 times a second which gives our brains rest,
according to some scientists, but also means, if you do the math,
we miss seeing for about 730 hours by the time we are fifty
not counting those times we close our eyes hoping to shut
others out.

       Near the Black Sea once, I watched three peasants
ride an ox cart down a dirt road towards the edge of the sky.
The light there seemed magnetic, the air seemed to converse
with eternity. I can't explain what that should mean now.
The youngest looked back as if to say these signs were enough
to tell me all I needed to know. The full white spade of the moon
had already started to dig into the earth behind me.

                      It was
near there that Ovid was exiled among what he called barbarians
who attacked his camp, but also his language for he feared he would
lose his words for love, for fellowship, for self. I think that's why
Kant thought that even God has to ask himself, Why am I?
It's a question, given the slaughters in Kenya and Syria,
Pakistan and Iraq, given the faces of the children who look into
the splintered faces of their parents who have been blown
into walls and car fenders, we don't want Him to answer, those
places where we don't want Him to even look.

                                                     What we see is
what we are. How many times have we wished only to notice
the way the lobster buoys bob just offshore. Or watched graceful
gulls follow the fishermen back to the docks? They seem sometimes
to hover there as if they have stopped time.

                                       But forgive me,
for now the sun has climbed above the horizon here without
incident. I remember the way we could trace the invisible
magnetic fields by putting a magnet beneath a sheet of paper
covered with iron filings. It seemed so simple, then, to believe
what we couldn't see. How many times is the world created
when, each morning, we open our eyes? Maybe History is what
we make of it. We live between what exists and what doesn't.

Now the cormorant seems to slide over the surface, content,
a bi-plane is dragging a banner whose message, too, has no special
meaning, except to say we are alive, that we see, when we want,
beyond the curvature of the earth, beyond our own lives,
and into the lives of those children because to see, finally, is
to love the invisible currents that bind us to one another.

RETRIEVALS
───────────

(2013)

The Gift

This plastic cup with the broken handle, green enough to
almost disappear in the grass by the roadside, has come
all the way from its origins in oil, and so it may be the last
gesture of some dinosaur or hold the last breath of an ancient
fern. About the size of a fist, it may have been tossed out
a window, probably a muscle car, perhaps thrown
in disgust at what was said on the radio news, or held
some bourbon before the driver spotted the police
cruiser behind him. Had he lost his job? Had his wife
left him for his best friend? It hasn't been here long.
The crows are busy with what's been pasted to the road.
Greasy wrappers, newspaper, even a used diaper
tell their own stories. The cup's probably made in China,
probably by some worker not paid enough to buy it.
Certainly the boys on the county clean-up detail would have
bagged it had they passed this way. If I leave it, perhaps
a mouse or an insect will make a home. We all need a home.
Just into the tree line the homeless tent village stays
out of sight. Someone there could use it. Maybe the one
who will thumb his way to Georgia for the onion harvest.
Or I could simply take it home to use as a planter to hold
the miniature, flowerless cactus my wife had left for me.

The Beach

From a picture of my father doing handstands, 1955

On the picture are scratches, or shards of light,
the detritus of invisible stars sifting through the clouds.
1950, the world as deadly as it is today what with beliefs
floundering around Korea, Berlin, McCarthy. So there's
my father and two friends doing handstands at Salisbury Beach.
It must be low tide given the distant, thin line of waves
behind them. The sky is wrinkled, the beach almost deserted.
Another war simmering in southeast Asia. He won't have to go
this time. It's as if their feet were holding up the sky
like caryatids. My father is the one with the shirt.
In twenty years, his brain washed clean, he will remember
only that. Back then he must be thinking the world makes
more sense this way. That's why he's looking away from us.

Epistemology

For Chris Buckley

They never end, our stories, though we try to tie them neatly
into sentences that yoke together like the box cars I can hear
slamming together in the rail yard to make a single train,
but they always seem to end up in some far-flung city whose
name escapes us. The stars assemble on invisible branches
waiting for us to name their shapes and we say *star thistle*
or *sunflower* to link the earth and sky. "True," we like to say
as a kind of assurance we know what we mean, but it's
a word that has the same root as *truce,* and even *tryst,*
though few of them are based on truth, and, more to the point,
the Old French word *triste,* a place to position yourself
during a hunt, or today, just plain sad. Maybe truth just takes
time to decipher just as a river takes ages to find the bottom of
the gorge, or the way a moth once thought its pupa was
a galaxy. And here—so much lies beyond the words
we do find: *cat's ear, horseweed, rattlesnake goosegrass,*
doveweed, skunk cabbage, crowsfoot, names that suggest
animals whose death has resurrected them as plants.
Tonight, I learned a name for our native grass: *lovegrass,*
wind dancer, what the Cherokee called it, and wondered
how many names are waiting to tell our own story.

The Truth

For Bret Lott

It's true, the shortest distance between two points is
not always a straight line. Nor between any of us.
It's true, our words are archives of what we don't
understand, maps of worlds we only imagine like one of
Einstein's thought experiments. What is the shape of love?
We can see it only by distant lightning that flashes
on the heart. It is not gravity that holds another's heart
inside our chests. There's a whole world beyond our mirrors.
It's true we have to choose between parallel universes.
In one universe the flowers forgive a trapped love.
In another they scourge the air we breathe.
One village has its hands cut off.
Another scavenges for airdropped food.
We make our walls out of our fears, it's true,
but we have to decide if it is to keep love out or in.
It is true, the wind is stuttering in the trees.
It cannot hide forever behind its calm mask.
It is true, the tracks of the fox outdistance its life.
We have to choose if the river's bones show
where the river dried up or where it will flood again.
These are signs we can read however we want.
Here are my shoes filling with tomorrow.
Here are my syllables turning to pure air,
speaking a language that is all disguise. It is true,
in Ezekial's Valley of Dry Bones it is the invisible
wind, the breath of souls, that brings new life
whenever we choose to love the worlds we name.

Cumberland Island

The live oak elbows its branches into the ground
to imitate our lives. Swallows carry messages
from lost souls. Some dreams never fly off, some
never sleep. Shawls of moss hang from the branches.
They lull you. The moon pushes up on a stem of light
over the horizon. The earth floats in its air. Orchids are
the oldest flowering plant with hundreds of species
each with its own pollinating insect. The future is
a salesman. We were looking for mushrooms.
History is just one path. The space between a word
and here puffs out like a milkweed seed. Our lives have
their wires crossed. Everything seems short-circuited.
The shadows of stars follow us even through daylight.
March, 1859, *The Weeping Time*, when Pierce Butler
auctioned off 436 slaves not far from here. There was
a time when we could mend these broken branches.
Syria still wanders around in its cage eating itself.
That metaphor shows how little I really understand.
I don't even know what the script says. The wind
seems lost. Where are the armadillos that should
have mystified me? The island is full of them.
Everyone wants to sell someone. Don't deny it.
God grows dizzy. Our words are sprinkled over our pasts.
You have to know the difference between the sound
of a star and the sound of a planet. Which one pollinates.
This page only exists if you happen to have read it.

Clouds, Myths

At 26,000 feet the clouds look more calloused.
It should be noted that no one knows what gravity is
and many theories about why a plane stays in the air.
These are the kinds of reality we once called myth
or superstition. Maybe we need our myths to blind
us the way volcanic ash cloud can blind a pilot's view.
Pliny said you can cure a scorpion sting by mixing
its ashes in your wine. Also, Magpies that feed on
acorns will learn to speak. At least that's what some
medieval tapestries suggest. And the unicorns on those
tapestries may stand for Christ. Marco Polo thought
the rhino was a unicorn. In one legend a unicorn's tears
heal a maiden's heart. At 20,000 feet the lightning
flashes buried in the clouds are either artillery flashes
or the thunderbolts of Zeus. Our own galaxy headed
for another galaxy. Each millennium the planets create
a new geometry of the sky. No one will ever decipher
the tapestry of our hearts. It's like those cold war maps
showing roads that don't exist to confuse some imagined
enemy. The ponds below us are strung out like mythic
tracks, perhaps of Anteros, the god of requited love,
which is all we can hope for. This is our final approach—
everyone on board dreaming of unicorns or gorgons,
the reality we can't have or the one we don't want.

The Word for That: Anghiari, Italy

For Tomaz Salamun

The trees are tempted. The moon is gagged.
Not everyone can live alone. On the *via dei Sette Ponti*
above Arezzo I tasted the light. What wasn't
to love? I thought the pollen were butterflies.
I discovered what della Francesca's Adam was keeping
secret as he watched his own burial. Their souls still
slither behind the paint. What does the river mean
by refusing reflections under *Ponte Buriano*?
Will the road correct itself? Will the wind believe
in itself once again? I am following the path
of some Roman legion. Tuscany is my fresco.
Everyone is his own saint. One sky sails behind
another sky. Stars pile up. Even the *cinghiale* have
their dreams. I can't remember the word for them.
I am writing you from James Wright's Anghiari.
It's true I am brooding because the statues are hungry.
They no longer know what they mean. Do we?
Even now the soul finds another workshop.
I meant the moon is a rudder with no boat.
I meant the trees were snares. Adam looked lonely.
I've settled into Castiglion Fibocchi to wait.
At least there is fruit on the table. At least
the sky blinks. Jupiter keeps tempting the moon.
Someone else will have to close our eyes.

RESONANCE

(2010)

Night Sky

Can you believe what the eloquence of these asteroids
tells us? That we are thrown through space from one
explosion to another? How amazing any love has endured!
In spite of the fact that so many tendrils of hope
wither in the sun, in spite of the way the flower now
seems to feed on the bees, that the lake seems to shackle
the sky, that the roots pull down the tree, in spite of the fact
that the clouds drag the earth towards some new final solution.
It doesn't matter where. There's a whole alphabet of hate,
a syntax of torture we can hardly understand. Petrified
promises take the day by the hand and lead her off
into some jungle. A couple of cigarettes walk towards
the dark end of a pier. A child's music shatters
like a broken violin. I used to think that any love we could
find is enough. It isn't. It isn't enough to plant our precious
gardens of hope in the sky. It isn't enough to write
by the fading candle of our eyes. It isn't enough to read
some future by the petals of the flower. Never enough.
We have to understand this love in the way the thorn defends it.
We can't let the moon rest its drowsy head on our rooftops.
We have to capture every wayward flash on the night sky and
not let our words burn up in the atmosphere. We have to follow
wherever they were heading. Sometimes I think we are all
hurtling through love at the speed of light. Maybe it is a question
of what galaxy we will crash into. Even now, you have to hear
what the arrow says before it strikes. You have to know
I will follow you over rivers of stone, even while you hold
my heart in your fist, that every love is filled with guilt, every love
tries to conquer a new world. I think sometimes we breathe
through the pores of the earth. It's the only way we know
the soul's body. It's the only way we can pass over the hobbled
roads of hate, the only way to shudder as the birds shudder
crossing the horizon. I am watching a bat scoop the emptiness
from the night, watching the hackberry embrace the moon.
Sometimes we have to hold hands with our own nightmares.

When I tell you that the voice of the nightingale turns dark
you have to understand what this love is trying to overcome,
you have to know that if you ever leave, if you ever disappear,
the sky would rip, and the stars would lose their way.

Write Your Name in the Space Provided

On any given day you'll meet me in the street.
On any given day our hearts may forget their own rhythms.
Today, for example, we worry about the glaciers
that are melting too fast in Greenland, meaning a future
that we are still trying to figure out. And we would be
wrong to think the sea is rising to greet us, or that our own
shores are too irregular to map. On any given day
the earth's surface rips somewhere like an old shirt,
what the scientists think the moon used to do before
any of our days ever existed. Do you think that is why
so many goddesses take the moon as their symbol?

Is that why the moon has become a sign for wavering love?
Sometimes I think the moon is a branding iron,
that we are all stamped with its indecipherable symbols,
meanings that are as lost as the creaking beds of
our lost dreams. On any given day our love can shift
the tides. On any given day our hearts seem to withdraw
into silence. But you would be wrong to think the heart is
a butterfly that disappears on the wind. No one knows why
the Anasazi of the southwest desert disappeared, but we can
still read the petroglyphs they left on hills so barren we translate
our own hopes, our own histories, into their given days.

Yet you would be wrong to think that on any given day
they need us to read them, or that the wind needs our maps
to follow, that the rain cares where it falls. You'd be wrong.
Not even the planets trust us to follow their paths. And
how often we think the Mockingbird is asking for us!
On any given day our names are shadows trying
to remember the skeletal shapes our words once took.
The wind conspires in the cellars of the heart. Out of love,
someone has scattered his enemies' skulls like rocks
on the desert floor. On any given day we are all
terrorists to someone else. At least the wind doesn't care

or won't tell the terrible things we've done. But you would be
wrong to think the heart doesn't try to conserve its love
like a dying star becoming its own red dwarf. Sometimes
you have to hold the sun in your arms till its shadow is your own.
You have to rub the stars like salt between your fingers
just to remember who you are. Every love is terrifying.
It's always a savage solar storm that creates the Northern Lights.
But today, today opens like a wound, and you are there.
And you would be wrong to think that when I reach
inside you I do not find the petals of your soul. You would be
wrong to think I wouldn't die for you on any given day.

Resonance

The hieroglyphics of sunset written on the bay's water:
your sad eyes the moon has lit its little fires inside of.
The wind untangling itself from streetlights and trees:
your voice hollowed out by a loneliness I can't name.
The heat lightning hesitating in the dark corridors of the night:
the meanings for your love that flicker like a worn neon bulb.
More and more these things shimmer on the spider's web
of despair. Resonance is what the scientists call it,
the heart's quivering responding to a nightingale's trill.
It's the way two molecules line up the exact same way,
or how two split beams of a light echo each other's
movements no matter what the other encounters.
Resonance. A far train sounds, a hunter's echo fills
the forest, and I shudder to think of a life without you.
The wake of a long-gone boat squints along the shore
and my love starts to ache like a phantom limb.
The screen here is filled with tiny worlds of water—
it's like looking through the thousand eyes of a fly
at a world where we can be everywhere at once.
It doesn't matter what seems to be only here. In Prague
you can see Albrecht Durer's "Feast of the Rose Garlands"
that's missing the fly he painted on the virgin's lap
some hack covered over in restoration. In this way
we understand how important it is to love every lost
detail—the phone numbers, gloves, scarves, checkbooks,
flowers, loves, glasses, stories, ear rings, keys,
the stones we walk on that echo an age we have forgotten,
the language you invent as you sleep, your words that ignite
the stars, your words that rise like birds from the trees.
What is it that you talk to in words that leave their shapes
like receding waves? Resonance: the way sounds echo
among interrelated counters in the head. I heard once
of fishermen who could hear the low rumbling sounds
from the hollowed heads of Croaker, Hardhead, fish you have
to answer to just to relieve your own loneliness. It's the same

way with seers who talk to stones. Because every word
we say means how alone we are. Maybe our memories are
useless, maybe our words won't save us. In Baghdad, Shiite
militia drill holes in the heads of Sunnis to make them talk.
I did not want to have to say that but it's a matter of resonance,
one thing leading to another the way a hang glider catches
thermals that keep rising, surrounded by hawks on the one hand
by vultures on the other. Now the heat lightning has stopped.
The wind rests its head on a branch. I don't know what else
to tell you. The cicadas' feet are stirring to song. Maybe
resonance is the texture of feeling, the depth of a look that is
something like the shadows stars cast on the sky. I am
imagining what you'll say, words like clouds avalanching
on top of each other, these little details, a glass of stout
that froths over, the wine stain on your lips, until one day,
all of a sudden it is today, now, and you turn to me, and speak
without talking, meanings that rise like steam after rain,
a touch like a cool cloth on the head of a dying man.

The Heart's Uncertain Myth about Itself

I'm not sure why I have begun with Aeneas' *Tree of False Dreams*
whose leaves fluttered lies, except that the mockingbird came
yelling out of the holly bush when I passed by as if he were
imitating the flight of Daedalus, and wanted me to follow
my own shadow into the dusk. I'm not sure why I didn't begin
with the Cyclops moth, whose eye spot is so huge its predators
think it's an owl, and flee. I'm not sure, except that sometimes
you have to invent a diversion just to talk when things go this way.

And I'm not sure why I just didn't begin by telling you how,
seeing the swallowtail there in the nettle, one leaf ripped against
a leaf's saw, was to find that name suddenly full of dusk,
or how, seeing that, I thought your skin was the delicate fiber
of its wing. In truth, a swallowtail darts about as if it were
a swallow. It leaves its eggs in the belly of a leaf beneath
some nightshade, knowing the odor of the larva will drive off
mud wasps, blackbirds, dragonflies. How much of any love

involves deception? Sometimes our words are like the sound
of bats in an abandoned steeple, a story our language tells us
before we know the meanings it disguises. The green frog
lowers its voice to scare off rivals. A shrike sends out false alarms
to scare off other birds. The blister beetle leaves its eggs in bunches
to imitate a female bee so the male will come, collect the eggs,
and bring them to the nest where they feed on honey and nectar.
They must feel like gods. They must feel they could fly.

Just above the horizon now, the kite of the full moon is caught
in the branches, larger than it will be all night. The last blisters
of light cling to the slate cliffs behind me. I'm still not sure why
I can never tell you what I mean. And that swallowtail—some females
darken themselves to imitate the poisonous pipeline butterfly.
And me, I lied about seeing it, for in truth there are none this far
north, except that I found the word so delicate, *swallowtail,*
I wanted to inhabit its sound as it settled on the leaf of your body.

Letter to Jo from Radovna Valley, Slovenia

If I would just from you, the wind would no longer hunt
along the cliffs, the light would no longer seemed forged.
If I would hear from you, maybe this sudden fear
would not have tracked me here where the air is still
bruised by these distant deaths. Sept. 20, 1944:
this house burned with all the villagers inside.
None of my words have echoes here. This is why
the future turns its collar up and walks away.

While I don't hear from you the universe is racing apart,
so we all grow more distant. I am fearful your life is
closing like this flower growing from the abandoned walls,
the way twenty-four souls in this house must have tightened
their fists. What did they hear before some roll of the dice
decided what village would die? Your doctor's dice are blank.
I think it's a dark planet that's growing inside of you.
Last night the cold earth wore the dark like your watch cap.

If I don't hear from you, each of these words will be a cave
lined with your handprints, the water beneath the bridge trembles
some memory from the other side of time. Centuries ago,
Dante saw the earth as a giant threshing floor. There's a giant
concrete hand here covered with the names of the slain,
the children turned to smoke. Now the birds are eating the daylight.
Sometimes I think we are all living inside this open wound.
Maybe this is why these dead open the windows of their souls for you.

Because I haven't heard from you I am telling you what thoughts
have broken the windows of sleep and ransacked my dreams.
But these metaphors are useless. They are vultures sitting on this house.
This is the architecture of death out of which we hope to construct
an architecture of life. We want the roots of the moon to reach the earth.
We want the wind to be made of doors. These are yours. You can enter
like a small star rebelling from the corner of the universe.
From one of these eyeless windows History leans out, its lungs

tightening, the words slipping back into its mouth. From this skeleton of a house the shadows still go about their daily business. The clocks are suffocating. My reflection in the water drifts downstream. The rounded roof of the kitchen rests like an unexploded shell. If I don't hear from you, I'll have to hide beneath the bark of the trees waiting for your name to be carved again. I'll have to wait like this snail shell trapped like the villagers for millions of years inside the stone if I don't hear from you.

Incompleteness

What would you call his feeling for the words
That keep him rich and orphaned and beloved?
                    —William Meredith, d. 2007

If we know Godel, we know every bird has a ghost in its mouth.
We remember we are dead so much longer than we are alive,
that there is always some truth we know but can't prove.
Some things will never stand for anything because they are
too much themselves. You can say the universe is
a blanket dimpled with planets and stars but you still
won't understand the gravity that shapes it. There is
always a beat of the heart the clocks don't count.
Some things don't even stand for themselves, as now,
when I'm trying to tell you about the death of a man whose soul is
the distant humming astronomers once thought they heard.
I can't worry about the way the scythe of the moon rips
through one darkness only to reveal a deeper darkness,
nor about the disappearing honeybees which threaten
our food supply. Anything complete is by definition
incomplete. Some things can stand for anything, as now,
trying to avoid these mentions of his death, it seems that
the borders of our souls are lined with watchtowers.
I can't ignore the small lights crying in distant windows.
I can't forget the bodies of the villagers in Darfur
who seem to stir the ground fog they still lie under.
Blackbirds dart like bullets across their sky. Every death,
he said, with that sideways smile, is ordinary. All I can do
now is talk to you about anything else. His words,
you once said, hung like a drop of water at the tip of a faucet.
Some things can't even stand for themselves. If we know
Godel we shouldn't worry if the single thread from the first star
spins out a fate we'll never understand, nor worry about
how easily any love darts in and out of the rafters, blind,
open mouthed to the darkness. The fireflies keep trying
to remember the stories they keep inventing. There are
desires waiting around the corner. There are desires
we haven't named yet, loves so impossible they have to be
true. We are always, he said, *rich and orphaned and beloved,*

which is to say the stars don't stop being startled by the dawn.
I can't worry now about any drought in our hearts. Each day
our bodies make 4,000 decisions we never know about.
Like Einstein we can imagine riding an endless beam
of light. Some deaths stand for every death, too much
to say: the nightingale's endless trills that are always searching
for us, saying that you are always on the frontiers of my heart,
that we don't need an alibi for staying, for now, among the living.

Here and There, October 7, 8:18 PM

Remembering Ken Smith

At 8:18 in the evening the mockingbird's cry began as an echo
of the only thing it wanted to remember. At 8:18 the windows hushed,
the breath whittled down to the only thing it knew. You can peel
away the heart layer by layer, but what remains is heart. I think
the hawks you saw once crossing the road in front of you were
practicing for that evening, leaving tracks on the air you knew
to follow. You once said that ash makes the richest soil, that we are
here to leave an extra syllable on anyone's tongue, that sometimes
a fish strikes before you have ever cast a line. At 8:18, the day before,
I watched tiny perch flipping across the surface of Lake Michigan
as if they were remembering a time they could fly. You'd have said
they had a quarrel with the sky. You'd have said they were warning
of a storm that had started ages before any of us were here.
It was a storm you must have seen flowering under the stars
of your Arizona desert. The roadrunners there, you once said, were
rushing to discover the short lives they didn't know they had.
At 8:18 that evening the mockingbird was waiting for the darkness
to hold its nest in its hand. I remember the last things you told me
from your hospital room phone, words that seemed to scratch
the sky with hope the way a prisoner etches his name on the wall,
a man who can barely see, outside, the neon sign with all but one letter
missing. Maybe we are all held under the shadow of a wing too
huge to grasp. Fish swim while sleeping, you said, we believe
in stars we never see, dots and lines on a screen that stand for
who we are. At 8:18 that evening a moth tested the mirrored
reflections in the room as if he were looking for a light that was true.
The heart circles back on itself like a man wandering in the desert.
At 8:18 that evening the sun had just set hesitantly. There was
a phone ringing reluctantly, there was the sound of a rescue copter
whose blades could lift the dust from the earth. There is the desert flower
that rises from that dust, the Palo Verde tree that thrives on drought,
stars that return each night to finish what they began. There is, you said,
a part of us that remains like the water stored for drought in a saguaro
cactus. And there are your words that still hide inside these words.
There are those invisible galaxies that continue to pull us towards them.

What It's Called: Skocjan, Slovenia

Jim Simmerman, 1954-2006

It's called the Shepherd of the Snakes, this black
butterfly with white spots. It's called *Heart in a Sling,*
this small, heavy flower reaching down towards the earth.
I learned this the other day from a man whose name dissolved
into this limestone earth. Learned, later, that I have been
living directly over the fault line of *Mala Dolina,*
the little sinkhole,' directly over the Reka river that appears
and disappears like a snake in the grass. Eventually,
everything we see commits a kind of suicide. Eventually,
every star becomes a heap of cinders floating aimlessly.
It's nearly 6 PM and I can hear the horses calling from
somewhere beyond the rock wall. You can smell the rain
in the air before it starts to rain, but there's nothing about
the soul's weather we can know until later. It's called
the soul's scar tissue, this distance from the dead.
It's called the *borja*, the wind that tears across
the stone roofs of this village at a hundred miles an hour.
Beneath me, a people whose names have been lost
for thousands of years took refuge by climbing into
the caves hidden in these cliffs. The floors there are
made of fallen roofs and hopes, broken histories.
It means we are always walking above ourselves down there.
It means we are walking above time. Above me now
Jupiter and Venus echo each other from two corners of
the sky. Beneath them the village graveyard holds the man
who mapped the caves. The dead keep dying within us.
It's like a drowned man's watch that still keeps time.
The early bats are tying the air, the heart, into knots. They
fly on the wings of grief. The late butterfly follows them
over the edge of the cliff where the earth becomes the air
we turn into. It's called mirror vision when we see what isn't
here. The kind of faith that fails at unexpected moments
the way a climber reaches for a hold that will never
in his life, be there. It's called despair
when we open the door of a heart that no longer exists.

Ten Things I Know

The brightest stars are the first to explode. Also hearts.
It is important to pay attention to love's high voltage signs.
The mockingbird is really ashamed of its own feeble
song lost beneath all those he has to imitate. It's true,
the Carolina Wren caught in the bedroom yesterday died
because he stepped on a glue trap and tore his wings off.
Maybe we have both fallen through the soul's thin ice already.
Even Ethiopia is splitting off from Africa to become its own
continent. Last year it moved 10 feet. This will take a million years.
There's always this nostalgia for the days when Time was
so unreal it touched us only like the pale shadow of a hawk.
Parmenedes transported himself above the beaten path of
the stars to find the real that was beyond time. The words you left
are still smoldering like the cigarette left in my ashtray as if it were
a dying star. The thin thread of its smoke is caught on the ceiling.
When love is threatened, the heart crackles with anger like kindling.
It's lucky we are not like hippos who fling dung at each other
with their ridiculously tiny tails.
        Okay, that's more than ten
things I know. Let's try twenty-five, no, let's not push it, twenty.
How many times have we hurt each other not knowing? Destiny
wears her clothes inside out. Each desire is a memory of the future.
The past is a fake cloud we've pasted to a paper sky. That is
why our dreams are the most real thing we possess. My logic
here is made of your smells, your thighs, your kiss, your words.
I collect stars but have no place to put them. You take my breath
away only to give back a purer one. The way you dance creates
a new constellation. Off the Thai coast they have discovered
a new undersea world with sharks that walk on their fins.
In Indonesia, a kangaroo that lives in a tree. Why is the shadow
I cast always yours?
        Okay, let's say I list 33 things, a solid
symbolic number. It's good to have a plan so we don't lose
ourselves, but then who has taken the ladder out of the hole
I've dug for myself? How can I revive the things I've killed

inside you? The real is a sunset over a shanty by the river.
The keys that lock the door also open it. When we shut out
each other, nothing seems real except the empty caves of our
hearts, yet how arrogant to think our problems finally matter when
thousands of children are bayoneted in the Congo this year.
How incredible to think of those soldiers never having loved.

Nothing ever ends. Will this? Byron never knew where
his epic, *Don Juan*, would end and died in the middle of it.
The good thing about being dead is that you don't have to
go through all that dying again. You just toast it. See, the real is
what the imagination decants. You can be anywhere with
the turn of a few words. Some say the feeling of out-of-the-body
travel is due to certain short circuits in parts of the brain. That
doesn't matter because I'm still drifting towards you. Inside you are
cumulous clouds I could float on all night. The difference is always
between what we say we love and what we love.
                                        Tonight, for instance,
I could drink from the bowl of your belly. It doesn't matter if
our feelings shift like sands beneath the river, there's still the river.
Maybe the real is the way your palms fit against my face,
or the way you hold my life inside you until it is nothing at all,
the way this plant droops, this flower called *Heart's Bursting Flower*,
with its beads of red hanging from their delicate threads any
breeze might break, any word might shatter, any hurt might crush.

Midnight

It's midnight because the windchimes have replaced
your voice. It's midnight because the porch chair
rocks as if you've just left it. It's midnight
because the dogs are barking at a raccoon. The moon
begins to limp across the sky. The coyote we saw
chasing those three deer must still be chasing them.
The streetlights shiver behind the branches.
It's midnight because suddenly there's this thought
of you that lurks in a distant doorway, a match
someone strikes ominously in the dark, a fear
that has no source and quickly shuts its eyes.
I can hear your name in what the trucks report
from the distant highway. The sky is in rags.
Storms of blackbirds. Sleepwalking stars.
It's midnight because that thought of you still stands
at the edge of these words like a soldier waiting
for an order, like a hole the unspoken word
drills in his heart. Because it's midnight,
I turn, terrified at this thought of you, turn
to our room, to you asleep on a sea of nightingales,
to lie beside the midnight of your own troubled
dreams, ashamed for my own foolish fears,
until the dawn shakes the darkness from the wings
of who we are and who we will always be,
until these words, wandering aimlessly, return
like the martin carrying its bright darkness to the feeder.

Morning Song

For my daughter Amy, getting married

Today it was morning all day, one of those little folds
in time when the ghost of the moon can rise without
a purpose, when the single thread of the soul seems
to pass through everything, gathering around us all
we love. Our own lives are invisible paths like
what the hawk followed this morning through
the branches outside your old window. He has found
a mate, and each spring they stay for a few weeks
to hunt and make a kind of love we can hardly imagine.
I think they have become acrobats of desire. Maybe
they are here to make us dream beyond ourselves
the way we want to know what's hidden behind colors,
or what rivers dream, or what the forgotten bulb dreamt
as it burst its way through the garden this early Spring.
Sometimes our words settle in the bottoms of our lungs,
and sometimes we fall into the deep well of each other
and find not darkness, not emptiness, not even the mossy
brick walls we expected, but a whole new universe of love.
This is not to deny that, as the scientists tell us, each particle
in our universe has a heavier twin, which perhaps accounts
for the darkness or heaviness we sometimes can become.
In a few weeks we will be in the grips of the early cicadas
creating another world in the trees, filling the kitchen
with trellises of song. Of all the lives inside us, we can live
only one. Of all the lives inside us, we want to find
another that keeps us astonished, like this one last star
that has forgotten to fade into dawn. Its light is tapping
on the window now. Sometimes it is you, sometimes
it is the love that nests inside you, and it dreams for us all.

HALF LIVES: PETRARCHIAN POEMS

(2004)

The Apology

Whoever hears in these scattered rhymes the raw sighs
my heart devoured when I was younger, or sees the soul's
tattered phrases hanging there unclaimed, don't scold
this art written by my other self, filled with confusion, not lies,
and forgive even this varied style I use now, that flies
as darkly as the crow, that scans the secret life of the mole,
that covers itself in Hope's blankets, that has always told
Love's truth, that now asks for pardon before its words run dry.
I know how rumor grew like a moth from a cocoon,
how some of you laughed when Shame stood at my door
for years, how Regret tracked me with her silent screams—
but also, and how each tree bears some fruit, how the moon
and the stars, the wind, the whole earth are images whose doors
open other worlds, if they only endure like the half-life of dreams.

The Prayer

Blessed be the year climbing its cliffs, the month crossing the fields
of hours and days, the bridges of minutes, the grass where we stood
that first moment, the festival music keeping our time, the hood
of the season's sky above us, the moment's fictive shield
against history, her tattered glance, her broken smile, everything real
or imagined, bless the rivers I invented to carry us, the woods
I planted as our own, bless even the sweet hurt, even the herd
of stars that trample my real heart which she has taught to heal.
Blessed be these trackless words running downstream
following the remote valleys she has cut through my life,
and blessed be the sounds they cannot make, but mean,
and blessed be all these pages watermarked with her name,
these thoughts that wander the unmapped roads of strife
and love, her blessed world whose dream is always a dream.

The Quandary

If this isn't love, then her heart's dealing from the bottom of the deck.
If this isn't love, then I've been given the wrong role in the wrong play.
If it is good, why does the sky seem to crack above me today?
If it is evil, why is my heart on the gallows, my soul on the rack?
If I burn by my own will, what heresy cast me into the fires?
If it wasn't my will, what good can any prayer accomplish?
Fate, choice, heart, soul, game, role or fanciful wish,
how does she have this power over me if I don't consent or conspire?
If I do consent—shut up, that's what I should do. I'm tumbling through some
emotional space like a new meteor, aimless, the proverbial
ship on a storm-tossed sea, smarter than some, dumber than others,
so I can't really tally the ledger on what's best for me or her
except to know I am poor without her, rich in memory, and begin to feel
death come each dawn, and most alive when my heart turns stone.

The Exile

Grief frames the doorway to that room I used to call my port
against whatever storms came careening down my street,
that room with its memories now crumpled on a table, a fleet
of hopes wrecked by words that regret what they alone distort.
Thorns fill the bed. A taunting night shakes its keys to closets
of desire I can no longer open. Who sleeps there, indiscreet
rival, while I flee his shadows that loiter like a disease
which waits for a soul to pummel, a love to perfectly thwart?
The doorknob of the night is always turning, but it is myself I flee—
my dreams, my rhymes, that lifted me towards a heaven
I thought was the love these words might finally create.
Maybe now I'll hide in those city crowds I've come to hate
since I can no longer face myself, no longer be alone.
Longing rings the doorbell, but the house is empty.

UNAUTHORIZED BIOGRAPHY

(2003)

Leap

World Trade Center, 9/11

It's when you see yourself sitting in your own grave.
It's when you remember those birds falling,
their lungs scorched by the Colorado fires,
leaving their unanswered calls drifting with the smoke.
It doesn't do any good to try rescuing some funny
word that has already plowed through
the loose stars rising to the surface of the evening,
a sky torn every which way by the earth's
gravitational field which some scientists say
looks like a deformed tomato.

It doesn't do any good to smile at that picture,
or at the joke someone tells you
about death being like missing the last exit
before the toll booth, or just a problem
with your complexion. It's because the tracks
of your own dreams have washed away into the gully.
It's because the heart burrows into itself for fear.
It's because someone noticed the remarkable red mist
that filled the air above the burst bodies of the leapers,
because someone noticed the lovers leaping backwards
out of the flames, holding hands, facing the sky
as if they might imagine themselves sitting
in some open field watching the fireflies in the woods
at Elkmont, N.C., mating, wavering in ribbons
like Northern lights through the forest.

But it doesn't do any good. It must have been
that way for the Italian soldiers who were found
among the icy rock crevices on the mountains
at Kobarid, Slovenia in 1919 because the seeds of the tomato
plants they were saving for Spring had sprouted
from their pockets, sprouted from their black limbs,
their skulls, their empty hands. It's when you think
of the abandoned glass photo plates you found

with your friend, of those gypsy sisters whose eyes
could have embarrassed the stars into silence,
a picture you have kept for 40 years
trying to imagine a life for her the way those leapers
and soldiers must have imagined their own lost lives.
It's when you remember your best friend has fallen
into the abandoned mine shafts of the years.

It's because, when if you do sit down in your own grave,
if you imagine, finally, a woman who thought
the moon was a scrap of light in your hands,
if you think of her grasping handfuls of wind
as the floor windows pass like broken film,
whose shadow finds a way to embrace the earth,
it is at that moment that a greater love comes to you,
a love made of everything you feared, everything
you despised, every death you tried to kill with words,
the seeds you still hope will climb like smoke,
the sprig of light that wavers in the distance,
the leap your soul takes towards an ambiguous moon,
the fireflies you hold in your fist, that you shake
like the stars from a place you will try to remember.

HEARTWALL

(2000)

Antigone Today

It turns out the whole sky is a wall.
It turns out we all drink from history's footprints.
One day the stones seemed to open like flowers
and I walked over the orphaned ground for my brother.
Even now I can count every barb in the wire.
The stars were covered with sand.
The sandstorm had almost covered the body.
I dug around him, covered him myself.
Today, each memory is a cemetery that must be
tended. You have to stand clear of the briars of anger.
You have to wash revenge from your eyes.
Sophocles kept seeing me as a bird
whose nest is robbed, screeching hysterically.
In another place a flock of birds tear themselves apart
to warn the king of what will happen to his state.
I don't know who I am. I hardly said a word.
I think Sophocles knew what I might mean,
and was afraid. Everything I did was under
one swoop of the owl's wing. Who is anything
in that time? And he never listened.
Even the sentry's words dropped their meanings
and fumbled like schoolboys forgetting their lessons.
What I dug up was a new word for justice,
a whole new dictionary for love. But why did my own
love desert me? He came too late. He was
another foolish gesture from another age. What I tried
to cover with dust was the past, was anger, was revenge.
Now you can see it all in mass graves everywhere.
You can see it in the torture chambers,
the broken mosques and churches, the sniper scopes.
You can see it in the women raped by the thousands.
Who is any one of us in all that?
Who was I? I've become someone's idea of me.
You can no longer read the wax seal of the sun.
The trees no longer mention anything about the wind.

I don't see who could play me later on.
It turns out I am buried myself.
It turns out we are all buried alive
in the chamber of someone else's heart.

Objects in the Mirror Are Closer Than They Appear

Because the dawn empties its pockets of our nightmares.
Because the wings of birds are dusty with fear.
        Because another war has eaten its way
        into the granary of stars. What can console us?

Is there so little left to love? Is belief just the poacher's
searchlight that always blinds us, and memory just
        the tracer rounds of desire? Last night,
        under the broken rudder of the moon, soldiers

cut a girl's finger off for the ring, then shot her and the boy
who tried to hide under a cloak of woods beyond their Kosovo
        town. Listen to me—we have become words
        without meanings, rituals learned from dried

river beds and the cellars of fire-bombed houses.
Excuses flutter their wings. Another mortar round is
        arriving from the hills. How long would you say
        it takes despair to file down a heart?

When, this morning, you woke beside me, you were mumbling
how yesterday our words seemed to brush over the marsh
        grass the way those herons planed over
        a morning of ground birds panicking in their nests.

When my father left me his GI compass, telling me
it was to keep me from losing myself, I never thought
        where it had led him, or would lead me. Today,
        beside you, I remembered simply the way you eat

a persimmon, and thought it would be impossible for each
drop of rain not to want to touch you. Maybe the names
        of these simple objects, returning this morning
        like falcons, will console us. Maybe we can love

not just within the darkness, but because of it. Ours is
the dream of the snail hoping to leave its track on the moon.
       we are sending signals to worlds more distant
          than what the radio astronomers can listen for, and yet—

And yet, what? Maybe your seeds of daylight will take root.
Maybe it is for you the sea lifts its shoulders to the moon,
       for you the smoke of some battle takes the shape of a tree.
       On your balconies of desire, in your alleyways of touch,

each object is a door opening like the luminous face of
a pocket watch. Maybe because of you the stars, too,
       desire one another across their infinite,
       impossible distances forever, so that it is not

unthinkable that some bird skims the narrow sky where
the sentry fires have dampened, where the soldier, stacking
       guns in Death's courtyard, might look up, and remember
       touching some story he carries in his pockets, a morning

like this blazing through the keyholes of history, seeing not
his enemy but those lovers, reaching for each other, reaching
       towards any of us, their words splintering on the sky,
       the gloves of their hearts looking for anyone's hands.

Do Not Duplicate This Key

It is not commonly understood why my love is so deadly.
At the very least it uproots the trees of your heart.
It interferes with the navigation of airplanes like certain
electronic devices. It leaves a bruise in the shape of a rose.
It kisses the dreamless foreheads of stones.
Sometimes the light is wounded by my dark cliffs.
Around me even the moon must be kept on a leash.
Whenever I turn you will turn like a flower following
the day's light. Sometimes I feel like Ovid's Jove,
hiding behind the clouds and hills, waiting for you
to happen along some pastoral dell thinking
what I might turn you into next. Then I remember
the way he turned himself into a drooling bull to scour
the pastures of Arcadia for Europa. Forget myth, then.
Forget Ovid. According to Parcelus, God left the world
unfinished from a lack of professional interest
and only my love can complete or destroy it.
Sometimes I come home, open a bottle of Chalone
Pinot Blanc and listen to the Spin Doctors'
"How Could You Want Him (When You Could Have Me)?"
My love is so deadly because it holds a gun to every despair.
But this is not the case everywhere. In some places
the heart's shrapnel shreds our only dreams. Even
the trees refuse to believe in one another. Sometimes
it seems we've put a sheet over Love and tagged its toe.
Someone thinks it lives in the mother of the Azeri soldier,
Elkhan Husseinar, because she puts, in a jar on his grave,
the pickled heart of an enemy Armenian soldier.
"This is love," she says, "this is devotion."
Someone else assigns Love a curfew. There's the 25-year-
old sniper who targets women in Sarajevo to see
what he calls "their fantastic faces of love"
as they glance towards their scrambling children.
This is when the seeds desert their furrows for rock.
This is when Despair pulls a Saturday Night Special

from its pocket and points it at the cashier in the 7-Eleven store.
This is when it seems each star is just a chink in our dungeon.
It is at this hour that I think entirely about you.
My love is so deadly because it wants to handcuff
the Death that has put all our lives on parole.
I myself escaped long ago from Love's orphanage.
I invented a world where the moon tips its hat at me.
I have this way of inventing our love by letting
my words rest like a hand on your thigh.
I have this way of gently biting your nipples
just to feel your body curl like the petal of a rose.
Even when I sleep you can detect my love
with the same instruments scientists use to see
the microwave afterglow of the Big Bang that created
the universe. My love is so deadly
the whole world is reinvented just as Parcelus said.
I love even the 90 per cent of the universe that is dark matter
no light will ever embrace. Rilke died from the thorn
of a rose because he thought his love was not so deadly.
My love is so deadly it picks the blossoming fruit tree
of the entire night sky. I can feel, in the deepest part
of you, the soft petals stir and fold with the dusk.
So deadly is my love
the call of the owl is thankful
to find a home in my ear. The smoke
from my cigarette thanks me for releasing it.
The tree changes into a flock of birds.
So deadly is my love other loves fall asleep in its throat.
It is a window not attached to any wall.
It is a boat whose sails are made of days and hours.
It rises like Botticelli's Venus from the sea.
This is not some idle myth.
In fact, it has been discovered that all life
probably began on the surface of deep-sea bubbles
which came together in Nature's little cocktail party
carrying most of the weird little elements we are made of,
the kind of molecular sex that excites chemists.
My love is so deadly it starts spontaneous combustions.
The whole universe grows frightened for what comes next.
The sky undresses into dawn then shyly covers its stars.

Sometimes I think your love is a compass pointing away.
Sometimes I discover my love like the little chunks of moon
they dig from under the Antarctic ice. My love is
so deadly it will outlast Thomas Edison's last breath
which has been kept alive in a test tube
in Henry Ford's village, Dearborn, Michigan. Even the skeptic,
David Hume, 1711–1776, begins to believe in my love.
My own steps have long since abandoned their tracks.
My own love is not a key that can be duplicated.
It knocks at the door of the speakeasy in Sarajevo
and whispers the right word to a girl named Tatayana.
This, of course, was from before the war,
before everybody's hearts had been amputated from their lives.
Now my love abandons all my theories for it.
This is why my love seems so deadly.
It is scraping its feet on your doormat, about to enter.
Sometimes you have to cut your life down
out of the tree it has been hanging in. My love is
so deadly because it knows the snake that curls inside
each star like one of Van Gogh's brush strokes.
My love is so deadly because it knows the desire of the rain
for the earth, how the astronomer feels watching
the sleeping galaxies drift away from us each night.
I am listening to your own rainy voice.
I am watching the heart's barometer rise and fall.
I am watching like the spider from your easel.
My love is so deadly, birds abandon the sluggish air.
Their hearts fall from trees like last year's nests.
The smoke awakens in the fire. The rose abandons the trellis.
My love is so deadly it picks the locks of your words.
And even tonight, while someone else's love tries
to scavenge a few feelings from a dumpster, while someone
lies across the exhaust grating like a spent lover,
my own love steps out from my favorite bar under
a sky full of thorns, weaving
a little down the sidewalk, daring the cabs
and after-hours kamikazes like someone stumbling
back into a world redeemed by
the heart's pawn tickets, holding a pair of shoes
in one hand, a hope that breathes in the other.

Reincarnation of a Lovebird

What's wrong with money is what's wrong with love;
it spurns those who need it most for someone
already rolling in it.
　　　　　—William Matthews

Already it is snowing, the branches spattering out of darkness
the way I imagine the nerve endings of that grasshopper
did on my sill last summer while the nightingale finished it.
Already old fears condense on the panes with you
a thousand miles or words away, my friend
recently buried, the light in my room blaring all night
the way it's done in prisons, trying to keep too much emotion
from scurrying out of the corners. There's a blind spot in
the middle of your eye, the guilt you feel for loving so fully
in the face of death, or dying in spite of love's power.
These verbs are searchlights for memories gone over the wall.
It's all we can do to embrace the distance between us
while night limps across these rooftops, while we preside
over the heart's fire sale. Outside the streetlights hook
a reluctant sky. Memory won't save everything.
That nightingale disappeared into the piracantha bush
to flute a melody we call imitation but may only be
another lie. Charlie Mingus' bass would die
into an arrangement, then reincarnate itself as a form of
love. It's time to decide if this is an elegy or a love
poem lurking behind one of the smoked glass windshields
that go up or down the street every few minutes. What we
should have said to each other waits like an insect
all winter for a false spring. The language of stars
no longer brings consolation or love. The Egyptians
invented the phrase, "eat, drink and be merry,"
you know the rest, but kept a skeleton
hung at dinner parties in case you tried to forget.
My love, the heart taps its way along sidewalks
like a blind man and muggers are gleeful on the corners.
What we need are more emergency vehicles for the soul.
We need to knock at the door of the heart's timekeeper.
The tracks I'll leave later when I go out into the purity
of snow will destroy it. The scientist's light
on the atom alters what should be there.
Every glass we raise we eventually have to lower.

You Can't Get the Facts Until You Get the Fiction

The fact is that the Death I put on in the morning is
the same Love I take off each night. The fact is
that my life slips out the back door just as I arrive.
Just now, just as I tell you this, while I am looking
for a little dignity under the open wound of the sky,
I am putting down the story of the two lovers killed
on a bridge outside Mostar. And the fact is love is
as extinct as those animals painted on cave walls
in Spain. The fact is, there is not a place on earth
that needs us. All our immortal themes are sitting
on the porch with woolen blankets over their knees.
But who wants to believe this? Instead, I am looking
for the right words as if they were hidden under
my doormat like keys. I would like to be able to report
that the nine -year-old Rwandan girl did not hide under
her dead mother for hours. There are so many things
too horrible to say. And I would like to tell you
the eyes of the soldiers are sad, that despite all
this madness I can still kiss your soul, and yes,
you might say I was angry if it were not for the plain fact,
the indisputable fact, that I am filled with so much love,
so much irrational, foolish love, that I will not take
the pills or step off the bridge because of the single
fact of what you are about to say, some small act
of kindness from our wars, some simple gesture that fools me
into thinking we can still fall, in times like this, in love.

No Turn on Red

It's enough to make the moon turn its face
the way these poets take a kind of bubble bath
in other people's pain. I mean, sure, the dumpsters
of our lives are filling with more mistakes
than we could ever measure. Whenever we reach into
the pockets of hope we pull out the lint of despair.
I mean, all I have to do is lift the eyelids
of the stars to see how distant you could become.
But that doesn't mean my idea of form is a kind of
twelve step approach to vision. I mean, I don't want
to contribute to the body count which, in our major journals,
averages 13.7 deaths/poem, counting major catastrophes and wars.
I'm not going to blame those bodies floating down some
river in Rawanda or Bosnia on Love's failures. But really,
it's not the deaths in those poems, it's the way Death arrives in a tux
and driving a Lamborghini, then says a few rhymed words
over his martini. It's a question of taste, really,
which means, a question for truth. I mean, if someone
says some beastly person enters her room the way Hitler
entered Paris I'd say she's shut her eyes like a Kurdish
tent collapsing under a gas attack, it makes about as
much sense. Truth is too often a last line of defense,
like the way every hospital in America keeps a bag
of maggots on ice to eat away infection when the usual
antibiotics fail. The maggots do a better job
but aren't as elegant. Truth is just bad taste, then?
Not really. Listen to this: "Legless Boy Somersaults
Two Miles To Save Dad," reads the headline from Italy
in *Weekly World News*, a story that includes pictures
of the heroic but bloody torso of the boy. "Twisted
like a pretzel," the story goes on. Bad taste or
world class gymnastics? Which reminds me. One afternoon
I was sitting in a bar watching the Olympics—the singles
of synchronized swimming—how can that be true?
If that's so, why not full contact javelin? Uneven
table tennis? The 1500-meter dive? Even the relay dive?

Someone's going to say I digress? Look, this is a satire
which means, if you look up the original Latin, "mixed dish,"
you have to take a bite of everything. True, some would
argue it's the word we get Satyr from, but I don't like
to think of myself as some cloven hoofed, horny little
creature sniffing around trees. Well, it's taste, remember.
Besides my satire is set while waiting at Love's traffic
light, which makes it unique. So, I was saying you have
to follow truth's little detours—no, no, it was taste,
the heroic kid twisted like a pretzel. Pretzels are
metaphysical. Did you know a medieval Italian monk
invented them in the year 610 in the shape of crossed,
praying arms to reward his parish children.
"I like children," said W.C. Fields—"if they're properly
cooked." Taste, and its fellow inmate, truth—how do we
measure anything anymore? Everyone wants me to stick
to a few simple points, or maybe no point at all,
like the tepid broth those new formalists ladle into their
demi tasse. How can we write about anything—truth,
love, hope, taste, when someone says the moment, the basis
of all lyric poetry, of all measure and meter, is just
the equivalent of 10 billion atomic vibrations of the cesium
atom when it's been excited by microwaves. Twilight chills
in the puddles left by evening's rain. The tiny spider
curled on the bulb begins to cast a huge shadow. No wonder
time is against us. In 1953, Dirty Harry, a "nuclear device,"
as the phrase goes, blossomed in Nevada's desert leaving
more than twice the fallout anyone predicted.
After thirty years no one admits the measurements.
Truth becomes a matter of "duck and cover." Even Love
refuses to come out of its shelter. In Sarajevo,
Dedran Smailovic plays Albinoni's *Adagio* outside the
bakery for twenty two days where mortars killed twenty two,
and the papers are counting the days 'til the sniper
aims. You can already see the poets lined up on
poetry's drag strip revving up their 22-line elegies
in time for the *New Yorker's* deadline, so to speak.
Vision means, I guess, how far down the road of your
career you can see. And numbers not what Pope meant
by rhythm, but $5 per line. Pythagoras (b. 570 BC)
thought the world was made entirely of numbers. Truth,
he said, is the formula, and we are just the variables.

But this is from a guy who thought Homer's soul was
reborn in his. Later, that he had the soul of a peacock.
Who could trust him? How do we measure anything?
Each time they clean the standard kilogram bar in Sevres,
France, it loses a few atoms making everything else appear
a little heavier. That's why everything is suddenly
more somber. Love is sitting alone in a rented room
with its hangman's rope waiting for an answer
that's not going to come. All right, so I exaggerate, and
in bad taste. Let's say Love has put away its balance,
tape measure and nails and is poking around in its tin
lunch pail. So how can I measure how much I love you?
Except the way the willow measures the universe.
Except the way your hair is tangled among the stars.
The way the turtle's shell reflects the night's sky.
I'm not counting on anything anymore. Even the foot—
originally defined as the shoe length of whatever king
held your life, which made the poets scramble around
to define their own poetic feet. And truth is all this?
That's why it's good to have all these details as
a kind of yardstick to rap across the fingers
of bad taste. "I always keep a supply of stimulants
handy, " said Fields, "in case I see a snake;
which I also keep handy." In the end, you still need
something to measure, and maybe that's the problem
that makes living without love or truth so much pain.
I'd have to be crazy. Truth leaves its fingerprints
on everything we do. It's nearly 10 PM. Crazy.
here comes another poet embroidering his tragic
childhood with a few loosely lined mirrors.
I'm afraid for what comes next. The birds' warning
song runs up and down the spine of the storm. Who says
any love makes sense? The only thing left is
this little satire and its faceless clock for a soul.
You can't measure anything you want. The basis of all
cleverness is paranoia. 61% of readers never finish
the poem they start. 31% of Americans are afraid to speak
while making love. 57% of Americans have dreamt
of dying in a plane crash. One out of four
Americans is crazy. Look around at your three
best friends. If they're okay, you're in trouble.

Basic Algebra

What does it matter if six is not seven?
Morning takes off its blindfold and the night
breaks into tiny roaches that scamper into
the crevices behind my refrigerator.
I refuse to pay such high prices for vegetables.
I don't feel any need to apologize for the number
of breaths I will take today. I have no
excuses for my age which has approached
the starting point of Zeno's paradox. Whenever
I see three at the supermarket, reaching
for more than he can hold, the legs and arms
of his clothes too short, he is distraught,
terribly distraught, that he is not eight.
Every number pretends to account
for more than itself. Therefore
the truth of every figure is a paradox.
Eight is the most sensual of numbers
writes Joachim of Avalon, platonic pimp
for the great Petrarch. When he pulls the chord,
the corporal at the howitzer has already
double checked his figures for elevation
though in the end he resorts to trial and error.
It was a mistake to keep this single knife in my heart
so long, but it is my knife, and my heart, too,
with its four distinct chambers. The only thing
that saves me is the certain fact that one is
not a number. It leans against the subway wall
afraid to go on. It listens to no one
and no one listens to it. I am going to
build a new nest for each of the birds in my throat.
For every kind thing you say, my father would
always tell me, a hundred kind things are
visited upon you. This is despite the fact
that somewhere someone is keeping
a second set of books about our lives.

Despite the number of howitzer shells
stockpiled inside our dreams.
None of this should enter our equation.
Maybe we should think of another number
besides ten which we can base our math upon.
Lately, despite the fact that some branches
refuse to offer a flower, despite the sky's
eating away at the horizon, I have been
thinking of eleven, which is also a lovely number.

The Poem That Was Once Called Desperate but Is Now Striving to Become the Perfect Love Poem

So then the sunken heart was hauled up, nearly breaking
the nets, and just at that moment, back ashore,
while the scandalous flowers were opening to the sun,
while Agamemnon had finished sending his messages
of condolence to his wife, the somber moon
began to exert unusual control over this sentence,
and I thought, wait a minute, what if this poem worked
and she began to love me? What if I could invent
a new word the way Catullus invented a word
for kiss? And would I have time to change those stars
that have been embalmed in the eyes of Agamemnon
to something like—well—but I know I *could*
think of something the way Clytemnestra's sentries
imagined every sunrise or glint of steel
to be the long-awaited signal fire.
Sentries, secret messages, royal scandals,
who am I kidding? When am I going
to stop living off the debris of lost loves?

But if it was to work, the poem, shouldn't I stop
wasting time and talk about something more
important in order to make her love me? There's
the Clytemestra syndrome to think about here
that is, the question of who lies best to whom.
And take Catullus—in one of his poems to Lesbia,
he talks about Troy and Herakles just to let her know
how cultured he is—yes, the mind, despite what we think,
it's *that* important—and then he mentions his brother
who died in Turkey, and he really did mourn a lifetime
for him, but the point is, he lets Lesbia feel his remorse too,
then sympathy, then—well, good sex, that was
Catullus' aim all along, wasn't it? And so with this
poem, surely there's time to add something about

my knowledge of the Trojan war, the complexities
concerning Agamemnon's murder of his daughter
and how I agree that, no matter how much the gods
commanded him, he should have turned around and
set sail for home and his anxious wife, all the while
emphasizing my essential sympathy with Clytemnestra's
plan to cut the bastard up like tonight's roast pork.

Maybe I should just go back to that little ship in the cove,
hauling up not a heart this time, but a statue, yes,
and an important find, good enough for a famous museum,—
but, well, maybe not, museums mean the past, death, lost
civilizations, lost love, so maybe a treasure—okay, ancient
Greek coins because this poem is set off some Greek isle,—
Agamemnon, remember—but wait, the trouble with dragging
in Agamemnon is that Aeschylus who wrote the play died
on just such a shore when an eagle dropped a shell on his head—
so maybe it's Sappho's island—this sticks better to my sub text—
where the poetess mourned for her lost love, and where—

But Sappho, you ask? Okay, true enough, but remember
Catullus also filled his poems with confusions of gender
to suggest the largesse of his sensitive and empathetic
vision to even the most difficult of lovers. Me too.
And why should I keep my hormones padlocked
in a single shed? Look what happened to Clytemnestra
waiting a decade for the one thing that drove her mad.
And why does everyone have to keep frisking the heart
for secret weapons? Why should I have to live like
there's an asterisk next to my love? Maybe the desperate
past is ready to weigh anchor, maybe my ideas are so plentiful
they'll just spill from the holes in my pockets like ancient
coins, and there she'll be, on that shore as the boat sails off,
happy like me, dressed like a Greek goddess, and she's ready
to spend a little time in my story, this story, with you
and me, where love is smuggled on board in containers
marked history, responsibility, prophecy, all those things
Desire's watchman never sees, decorum, reason, reality,
and all the other contraptions we use to try to avoid them.

No-Fault Love

No one seeing the suspect, Richard Jackson, should ever
try to approach him. His description contains as many
contradictions as Proteus. The heart's cabdriver
reports that he has fled into tomorrow because he is so
tired of speaking about yesterday. If you do not
recognize his crime you are already an accomplice.
The remarkable thing about tomorrow is that everything is
the opposite of today. The shadow that now stalks you
becomes your confessor. And it is true, desire never
loses its grip on tomorrow. But just because tomorrow
follows today does not necessarily mean that one thing
always follows another. The bullet that is heading
for your heart may never arrive, the plane floundering
towards earth may even pull up at the last minute,
given the ambiguities and uncertainties of tomorrow.
None of tomorrow's verbs can ever finish what they're doing.
Trees stand for anything. Stars, too, stand for anything.
The whole galaxy screams something that is soon forgotten.
So you can forget about the Bosnian bells with their
human tongues. The business of tomorrow is pulling up
the roots of sadness so that the three children
blown up in the speed factory in San Diego—
what am I saying? We want to live as if our own bodies
were nests. But possibility opens like the palm of
a waving dictator. You can scale the ruins of heaven
in search of love and never find it. But if you find
Richard Jackson tomorrow, or even the day after,
approach with caution—his words are snares.
The horrible thing about tomorrow is that today is already
history. We don't even exist the way we exist.
Truth becomes a fixture. Love wakes in the keyholes.
I don't know what other clues to give you.
All the good souls have fallen from their nests.
By tomorrow, the scene of the crime will be forgotten.
But the heart, the heart's fingerprints are everywhere.

Heartless Poem

It is true that my heart does not exist.
It is absolutely true that the birds are not mine,
the river will not stop for me, the leaves will not
stop aiming for the very ground where I stand,
that I cannot hold the smallest amount of air
in my hands. The closed fist of the moon
punches its way through the lake.
Someone else might talk about the moon as a heart,
but that's all I'm going to say about it.
On this night when the stars begin their lies
about the light beyond them, when the young men
from Tuzla are hanging from lamp posts
instead of lights, I am here to tell you
my heart has never existed.
The only feelings I have ever heard of
take to the highway with the carts
and trucks of the other refugees.
Why do you think you need to join them?
If it were a violin my heart would not rest
between anyone's chin and shoulder. It would
sit in a pawnshop window for someone's supper.
On this night when my heart does not exist
I eat out of the hands of yesterday.
If it did exist, the fist of my heart would
grab the hanged man by the collar of his soul
and turn him away from his own death.
But who can say anything about the soul?
The soul, too, is just another migrant.
I have heard that the soul and the heart are
the two best scavengers of whatever past
you have discarded by the side of the road.
You can find them sneaking around in some orchard
behind the smoke a farmer uses against the frost
or plucking the hanged man's weight like a pear.
See, it is not so hard to say something about nothing.
The stars are already leaking their light into dawn.
But I can tell you that my own heart has never existed.
That's all I'm going to say about it.

Sonata of Love's History

Before I could arrive at this moment when the earth
wakes inside you, when the night is still tangled in your hair,
before I could see how the moonlight melts
on your breasts as you lay beside me,
before you opened the hands of your soul,
at this moment that is so sudden, so unexpected,
I can only imagine how the softness of your voice must be
enough to stop the insects for miles, and I begin
to understand how the way you open your eyes
to the morning must be enough to change orbits of planets,
so it must have been necessary for me, if I've really arrived
at this moment alive, to have lived
a life where only my shadow planted the garden,
only my shadow walked through the market,
fingered the keys nervously, drove the car too fast,
and it must be the same shadow that curls up
in the corner of the room or is hung in the closet
collecting moths, and it must have taken centuries
of bones turning to light, of rivers changing course,
of battles won or lost, of a farmer planting one crop
or another that failed or not, one atom hitting
another atom by chance, and through all this a single
string of time survived volcanoes, lightning strikes,
car wrecks, floods, invasions to lead to this moment
abandoned randomly to us, this singular moment that is
part of time's litter or maybe its architecture, because now
in this moment which is so wondrous the way
it lies beside you, I either do not exist or the past
has never existed, either my breath is
the breath of stars or I do not breathe as I turn to you,
as you breathe my name, my heart,
as the net of stars dissolves above us, as you wrap
yourself around me like honeysuckle, the moon
turning pale because it is so drained by our love,
so that before this moment, before you lay beneath me,

you must have disguised yourself the way the killdeer
you pointed out diverts intruders to save what it loves,
pretending a broken wing, giving itself over finally
to whatever forces, whatever love, whatever touch,
whatever suffering it needs just to say I am here,
I am always here, stroking the wings of your soul.

Things I Forgot to Put on My Reminder List

Turn off the coffee. Feed the cat. Lock the door.
Don't let the morning drift away like a barge.
Don't let sorrow drain the stars from the pond.
Don't try to colonize a lost past. Words like icebergs
breaking loose from the pack. The grammar of loss.
The heart being cannibalized. The mangrove of despair.
What else have I forgotten to pack? Everything
flares up in this fire like a pine cone dipped in wax.
The leg of the walking stick goes up like a match.
The light grabs everything like a hungry star.
How do we ever know what is important enough
to remember? History's promises knifing us in the back.
The snipers who have started to reload.
If only we could see them in those hills.
Why is it raining inside all the clocks?
The importance of remembering: of the nearly five
thousand heartbeats per hour, only one has to forget.
The shifting arguments of artillery positions.
The firelight falling, the embers forgetting the flame.
Those men in the Bosnian hills forced to bite off
each other's testicles. The souls carried there
in satchel charges. Hate dripping off the table
into the next century. What will be left for any of us?
Fix the screen, wash the car. Mow the lawn. To watch
the snail making its way up the side of a house
all night, leaving a history only we can understand.
Or the sky that lies shattered at your feet. To
peek through the keyhole of fate. To see how
the night still lingers in your eyes. The way my soul
levitates around you. The smell of over ripe
peaches on the counter. How you open your eyes to me
in the morning. Maybe I should just crumple this list
into the fire. Maybe our hopes can no longer fly
like those two wild turkeys we saw yesterday.
Apples, coffee, juice. Is there any part of you

my mouth has not touched? My old self hanging
like a moth-eaten coat in a closet. Call the florist.
Mail the letters. Pick up the tickets. Check the maps.
Don't worry that the earth's inner core spins faster
and laps us every 400 years. We are still here.
In spite of. In what way. In the meantime.
The wasps chasing us, getting caught in your hair.
The assassin's night scope needing adjustments.
Time: the black ants eating the tree from the inside
out, always anticipating, always dreading
the moment they see light. Where would we live?
Don't worry, the heart always floats to the surface.
The essence of string theory in physics being
that we are all tied together by invisible emotions.
These words at your door like a nervous delivery
boy. Everything wants to take flight. The sparks
of this fire disappearing into the dark. The names
of the victims always written out of the treaty.
Where can we go with our squeaky fan belt,
our retread tires, our out-of-date maps?
Inside you, all roads unravel. Even before I touch you:
how you start to imitate the way the ground fog
wavers across the grass. Some nights the dew
seems to soak the stars. Your laugh settling
in the corners. Your words weeding the flowers.
The old doubts finally washing up on shore.
Paint the house. Trim the bushes. Patch the roof.
Get rid of the garbage. Return the calls. Turn off the lights.
Bandage the heart. Bandage the hour. Hold you
against the sky, against the future.
Each of us shadow boxing with eternity.
To let your voice halt the moon in its tracks.
To lean out over the balcony of desire.

ALIVE ALL DAY

(1992)

The Italian Phrase Book

Good morning. Good day. Good afternoon. Good evening.
I am happy to meet you. My name is Richard.
Here is my passport. I have nothing at all to declare.
There is a message for you of the greatest urgency.
Where is the nearest taxi stand? the nearest telephone?
To the right. To the left. Straight ahead.
You can walk there. You can take the bus.
Someone is missing. Word of him can be heard
where the cricket songs are igniting the grass.
Please consult your phrasebook for the proper response.
Two blocks on the left. Turn right. Do you have anything
I want? How much will this cost? Will you have something
to drink? You can point to the proper question or answer.
While you are waiting, let us take a closer look at the town.
Here is the wonderful Roman coliseum. What do you know
about the early martyrs—who wavered before the lions,
who wept, ashamed, into their own arms? You do not have
to know the exact words. The wind from some far place
does not have to fill your shoes. How much do I owe?
There is one item missing. There is a defect in the sleeve.
Can we agree on a price? The theater where Catullus played is
on the other side of the Adige. Here is the famous Church
of the Veronese martyrs. Here are the famous tombs of the Medici.
You will see others built high into the sides of buildings.
But just a minute. Hold on. Wait. This phrase book cannot
answer everything. This guide book is not really like being there.
What does it tell you about the years Dante
spent exiled here from Florence? For him it was all assassins,
and the heart's gravediggers who abandoned
their half-completed holes to the dark. For him it was
the moon sweating in the fields outside the walls.
If you wish, we will turn to a different category.
Look, here is the supposed tomb of Juliet. The lovers have
dropped their notes in languages we might be able to translate.
You should consult our other books in this series.

We won't even bother with the language of lovers.
But this is a good time to practice ordering her wine.
We suggest the local Soave or Pinot Grigio while you wait.
It seems your urgent news is being delayed in another language.
This is a good time to toast your love. You may mention
the uncut meadow, the haystacks waiting to take shape,
how all the roads to the past have been closed,
how each night she tightens around you with the dark.
Can you find the Piazza Erbe with its famous umbrellas
and market? You will find fresh peaches and pears.
You will find fresh oranges. Here you will be able
to practice many phrases. Be careful about numbers.
Nearby is Juliet's balcony. There are street corners,
whole towns not shown on your map. There are the dead
who still lean against the buildings without the proper facts.
There is Love crouched beside the stalled car on a side street.
Without practice all your new phrases will evaporate
from the city streets like rain water. Don't worry.
Here is a night's growth of fog, covering the fountains,
disguising the few tourists who are still out, like you.
Here comes night wrapped in a shadow of remembered scents,
stopping at my bench, opening her sack for me.
What is this made of? Can we agree on a lower price?
Using these idioms you will soon sound like a real native.
Can you help me find what I want? How far is it?
In the Gobi Desert scientists have unearthed an 80 million
year old lizard never before known to man.
Beneath the market they have found an Etruscan village.
Would you care for another glass of Pinot Grigio?
It is said in today's paper that all news of our universe
travels the crest of nearly imperceptible gravitational waves
which we can decipher only months later. It was in this square
that the Roman priests would read the entrails of strange birds.
So it seems that only later will today's news reach you.
It seems the phrases are filling with desert and salt.
It seems the crows have been unspooling across the Piazza Bra
for an hour, the very hour your friend has turned his car
into the wrong lane half a world away. What is the tense for this?
What is the proper word? You may repeat these phrases.
I feel sick. I have got to see a doctor. I am only a tourist here.

I have an ear ache. I have a terrible headache. I have a toothache.
I feel nauseated. It hurts here. It hurts there. Yes, I would like
to take something for it. When should I call again?
Our connection was cut off. It was a country road,
the other car coming through the fog over a hill.
It was late afternoon. He must have been reciting
his favorite Byron, his favorite Dante, turning their grief
into love, making love songs of their elegies. It is not possible.
I have this headache. Just a minute while I transpose the sum.
Sign here. The tip is included. Is this enough? Just a minute.
Here comes despair picking up the used cigarette butts.
Here are the old memories crouched in the door stoops.
If you cannot find the correct phrase,
try combining elements from the ones you already know.
This is the moment you must remember how the songs of lovers
pass from one bird to another and become pure joy.
Even the sky is prepared to lie about its moods.
What is your shadow doing there, bent over against the wall.
Please consult the phrase book for the proper response.
Please listen, then repeat the following lines.
My love, whose fingers are matches, whose waist is
encircled by the arms of the wind. My love, how the world
sleeps in your throat, how your heart is filled
with the scents of raspberries and grapes,
to live inside you, to live inside the warm peach.
Otherwise there is no way to stop despair from lurking
all night in the shadows beside the old toll gate.
Otherwise we will have to weep in another language.
In that case, all our words will fall in love with gravity.
Otherwise we will have to stop taking breaths
from this moment on. From this moment on
the stopped clocks will observe us. My love,
our hearts are growing full of broken wings.
My love, to find our voice in a drop of water,
in the tracks the moonlight leaves behind.
If only this were enough. If only the news.
Even the sky. The sky. It hurts here. It hurts here.

The Angels of 1912 and 1972

It is a long time since I flapped my wings,
a long time since I stood on the roof of my house
in Lawrence, Mass., or Michael's in No. Andover,
a little whiskey in one hand, the past slipping
through the other, a little closer to the heaven
of dreams, letting the autumn wind, or the spring
wind, or maybe just the invisible breath of some
woman lift me up. It is a long time since I have flown
like a swallow, or even the clumsy pigeon, into another
time, practicing miracles, dodging the branches
of lost words that cut against the sky,
and the rocks thrown by small boys, finding
the right nest under the eaves of some pastoral age
even the poets have forgotten, or fluttering
to a slow landing on some ledge above the buses
and simple walkers of this world. It is a long time.
From where we stood I could see the steeple of the French
church. Further back, it was 1912, and I could almost
see the tenements of the French women who worked
the fabric mills, weaving the huge bolts of cloth,
weaving the deadly dust into their lungs.
They could hardly fly, these angels. I could
almost see them marching down Essex Street and
Canal Street to the J.P. Stevens mill, the Essex Mills,
pushing against the police horses for two bitter years,
thousands of them, asking for bread and roses, asking
something for the body, something for the soul.
If I did not fly so far I could see my mother's father,
years later, stumble to the same mills, nothing gained.
Or I could have looked ahead to this very year, and seen
Bob Houston and I standing on a roof in Bisbee, Arizona,
two desert sparrows flying blind against the night
once again, remembering the union workers herded
into boxcars and shipped from there into the desert
a few years after my French weavers flew down

Essex Street. But it was 1972 and we still believed
we could stop the war with a rose, as if there were
only one war and not the dozens of little ones
with their nameless corpses scattered like pine cones.
It was 1972 and we stood on the roof like two angels
lamenting the news that John Berryman had leaned out
over the Washington Avenue bridge in Minneapolis,
flapped his broken wings, dropped to the banks below him.
"I am a nuisance," he wrote, unable to find a rose for his soul.
We thought we could stand on that roof in 1972, two
Mercuries waiting to deliver his message to another time.
I should have seen what would happen. I should have seen
my own friend on his bridge, or the woman who could have
descended from one of those French weavers leaning
on the railing of the north canal in Lawrence because
all hope had flown away, or my own father starting
to forget my name that same year. If there is anything
I remember now, it is the way he looked at me in his
last year, wondering who I was, leaning back against
his own crushed wings, just a few years after he told me
to fight the draft, to take flight, or maybe he leaned
as if there was a word no one would ever speak
but which he knew I would believe in, that single word
I have been trying to say ever since, that means
whatever dream we are headed towards, for these
were the angels of 1912 and 1972, the ones we still
live with today, and when you love them, these swallows,
these desert sparrows, when you remember the lost fathers,
the soldiers, when you remember the poets and weavers,
when you bring your own love, the bread, the roses—this is flying.

Victor Hugo's *The Hunchback*
of Notre Dame By Richard Jackson

There's a door that begins with a hole in the heart.
There are these old feelings I carry on a chain.
There are little cloisters of darkness in the light.
There is the desire of the rain for the willow's roots.
There is a cathedral—I was elected "The Pope of Fools."
Its gutters are too small to capture the overflow of history.
Light lances the windows like a Roman soldier.
There must be sounds, but they have folded
themselves into petals for the night.
There's someone who will leave the door open
so Death walks in chomping his cigar like a union boss.
There is Esmeralda who gives the moon its light.
For now Death just opens the refrigerator door
letting the light spill out as if it were milk,
reading the old novels he's insanely devoted to.
There's a storm breaking out deep in his mind
There's the archdeacon falling from the drainpipe.
There's Victor Hugo who spent 20 years in exile.
You can see Rodin's statue in a Park in Paris.
He tied the rope around the gypsy's neck.
She wasn't a gypsy. She was an angel.
When she danced he thought she was a witch
for what she made him think. Why is the world
always passing beyond the rim of our eyes?
Why would anyone think she was a witch?
There's a woman in New Mexico who saw
the image of Jesus on a tortilla she burned
in a skillet in 1977. There's Arlene Gardner
who saw him on her freezer in East Springs,
Tennessee, ten years later. Now they are saints.
Why is the sun always asleep in your heart?
There's this face, this body, no one can argue.
But there's Tycho Brahe who wore a metal nose
from a duel. All he could do was measure.
He understood nothing. He shook the stars

like dice to guide him. Now he's a saint.
He died from an infected bladder
because he was too polite to leave the table.
There's the way my gypsy hung against
that roulette wheel of the moon. There are
the years I lay beside her sifting into dust.
There's casual breeze rolling a few cigarettes in the alley.
And there's Death, it's your door he's entering now.
He's playing jacks for the random moments
you have already forgotten. You thought
you could take off the past like a pair of socks.
There's the blood in his veins which is smoke.
There are blackbirds disguising themselves as stars.
There's the way he throws finger shadows
on the old calendar tacked to the wall
trying to imitate the shapes he's taken
against the cathedral door. My own spine
happens to aim at the sky like a dogwood.
There are the hoofs of someone else's story
always clattering through the city gates.
There's the rain bringing its memories
of what happens higher up.
The dust is already settling in my dreams.
There's a suitcase beside a road afraid to go on.
I'm not saying it's mine. I'm not saying it's yours.
There's all those dying planets gnawing on their bones.
There's a little stain of blood on the floor of heaven.

About the Dogs of Dachau

I'd even given you part of my shared fear:
This personal responsibility
For a whole world's disease that is our nightmare.
                              —Sidney Keyes

About the hearts of dusk that could make
pets of dogs the Nazis abandoned as they fled.
About turning to answer the dust devil
scuffed up by the wind, thinking I heard your voice,
and seeing the Rottweiler rise, alarmed, from the gravel.
About the Shepherd out near the disinfecting shack
nosing decades-old scents along the inner fence.
Also, about Mr. Valincourt's Doberman,
another summer, 1956, the olive
drab coat I borrowed from my father
caught on the chain link fence where I played army.
About that lost world where I carried death
on my shoulders, where the moss on the moonlight
said nothing yet about the piles of dead shoes.
Nothing of what I want to tell you.
About the dogs clamoring at the sound of a distant train,
about the shell casings of words we wanted to forget.
About this place.
About the fragment of a mouth organ
I found along the stream that is
still crossed by barbed wire. About the way
it freezes in winter and the man caught on the wires,
1941, the museum photograph says,
a spider's pod of snow wrapping around him.
About this place.
About our love in a world where the air is swollen,
where clouds only bruise the sky,
where stars refuse to connect as constellations.
About the coats heaped in a pile at one end of the camp.
About the lice, so many they could move an empty arm,
as if each coat were alive.
About those coats you can still hear
on a camp bench, maybe looking over a makeshift
chessboard and through themselves at the tourists.
About how clean this place is. The past

trying to stay only in the past. About the unbelievable
postcards, showing collections of rings,
hair, teeth, the body's trash dump.
Why I sent you the blank card from here.
Why my terror went looking for clothes,
poking like a searchlight through rags of words.
Why I wanted to hold you until we turned into birds
because here it is only the birds that are not branded by fire,
because they can turn into specks, then stars
so distant we can never disturb their light.
About the swamp at one end of the camp,
and the town at the other where the smell must have drifted.
About no one wondering. About the cries of the dogs
interrupting the still nights in that town.
About the old questions darkening the trees of the town,
and about the old answers lighting the tree tops.
About these sentences that cannot stop
at the horizon. These words with their nervous jugulars.
About everything returning, as Nietzsche threatened it would,
the pack of shadows crossing the yard like dogs,
the one turning to snarl like Mr. Valincourt's Doberman
at the coats who must stand for hours in the yard nearly naked,
at the execution procession with its slumped coats
stumbling through the mud, forced to play
the grotesque violins and trombones for their own deaths.
About this mouth organ, if that's what it is,
the rust and wood crumbling like a badly remembered song.
About how the inmates put on the night, the day,
how they put on tomorrow, the erratic flight of a butterfly
that has escaped the snapping dogs,
put on even the flowers, the trees, the windows,
how they put on the camp weather vane
which is another name for the soul.
About this tabloid I bought pointing to the frog boy,
kept alive by authorities like a huge tadpole,
peering out from his home in Peru.
About the huge coat he tries to hide in like a pod.
About wanting to kiss those eyes
bulging from his forehead, the flipper arm
reaching out as if to brush a fly. About the dogs, the town dogs
that go crazy when he is wheeled out to the yard.
About the dogs of Dachau,

how they sleep beneath the barracks like pools
of water that do not reflect the sky,
how their cries stiffen the coats and rub the eyes of morning.
About one of these coats, Esad's. About the way
he slumps in his bunk, peering out like the frog boy,
the dysentery leaking from the bunks above.
About his festering foot sticking to the straw.
His experimental foot observed by the camp doctor.
About how even the starlight shakes the wind
carrying the screams from high altitude experiments,
cold water experiments, malaria experiments,
and how the echoes of the dogs sniff through
the abandoned ghettos of the heart.
About the woman. The way, each night,
he would tremble before her in his own skin
like a cypress whose sparrows are
stirring to leave. About skin,
about flesh, because it is so alive taking flight.
About the way he dreams us, the way the coats
in those camp photos dream someone will wonder,
decades later, who they were. About his dream of
the way I rise from you, slump to the side like he does,
and the way you cry, the way we both cry maybe
just because we can make the stars into constellations,
because we have skin to touch and to cover.
About the simple coats we put on, putting on the world.
About this small mouth organ he must have refused to play.
a few keys tuned too high at one end for the dogs.
About fashioning it out of splinters from the bunks,
of metal from the camp shop, of the sky
that shrugged above his childhood in Istria,
the broken wings he fixed, the pain
of the quarter moon afraid it couldn't go on.
About the pockets it was carried in, the old faces
that crowd onto it like a sinking boat,
to snap it against the palms of our words,
so that the leaf will not have to face its death alone.
so that the whole landscape will turn into music,
this small mouth organ, this graveyard of voices,
from which no song must ever be finished.

Homeric

She just hauls out and smacks him
on the side of the head which sends him reeling
against the plate window of the Krystal
hamburger shop while the old couple inside,
she in the print dress, he in the light orange
polyester suit, just watch because they've seen this
a hundred times, maybe a thousand, and there's never
any reason to speak of, so that the boy just
straightens up, lowers his head, and walks
behind his mother. The old folks are there because
the Krystal hamburgers are steamed and soft
to their gums, and me because my new root canal
won't take too much pressure yet, and the mother
and son because there's not a hell of a lot to do in
Chattanooga, the bible belt, on a hot June morning, 1989.
There are a couple of choices—you can walk away,
letting the scene continue for generations and make, if you
know words, obscene art from someone else's pain;
you can abduct the kid in a dramatic rescue, which will
add to your pain and his; you can lecture the mother
in which case she'll take it out on the boy; or maybe
slap her silly, which is what I would have done
thirty years earlier, the year I discovered Homer's
rosy fingered dawn, as preached by Sister Michael,
was really the bloody one Hector, Ajax and the others
made for themselves, and the one I knew then
on Lawrence and Haverhill streets—the chains,
the black taped flashlights, the kick boxers,
the knuckles, the whisper of zip guns—the year I had
enough of it from Charlie Pilch and his brother, and
so pushed them against the chain link fence, amazed
as they were at how fast my fists were hitting them
until they fell bloody beneath me, no Homeric dawn,
no heroic fight, and then ran home to get sick
for my own stupid cruelty. I don't know how

I escaped that world where you were either lucky
or nearly dead, where we drank Hollihan's ale
behind the brewery when the night shift sold us
illegal, and we argued how we should have joined
the Hungarians throwing bottles of gasoline at Russian
tanks, not for nobility of freedom, but because that was
the way, how we should have dropped the bomb,
beat it out of any one who said we couldn't. I don't
know if the world I've entered is much better
because I'm clenching my fists inside my jeans,
biting so hard it's only my foolish and rootless
tooth that warns me back from the woman,
and I have looked over the rough idea of the world
this has become, the endless cars making their way
down Brainerd Road with their own gritted angers
to face, the polyester man snapping at is wife,
the hot sun which is just another star angry with itself,
the street preacher who's taken up his cross
with its bloodied spots for wrists and ankles, not
even him, none of them even noticing that boy
who has already walked off the world of poems,
who may or may not be lucky enough to escape
this or that world, drive his car, some used junk,
out to the levee or dam, look back over the city
lights that are okay even if they are not the tent lights
of the noble Greeks on the plains of Troy,
where he will remember from that safe distance,
like some Achilles still brooding over a small loss,
how his life, too, almost came to an end
on several occasions, some worth it, some not.

The Other Day

On the other hand, to no longer wish oneself
to be everything is to put everything into question.
—Georges Bataille

I just want to say a few words about the other
day, an ordinary day I happen to recall because
my daughter has just given me a yellow flower, a buttercup,
for no reason, though it was important that other day,
that ordinary one when the stones stayed just stones
and were not symbols for anything else, when the stars made
no effort to fill the spaces we see between them,
though maybe you remember it differently, a morning
when I woke to find my hand had flowered on the breast
of my wife, a day so ordinary I happened to notice
the old woman across the street, hips so large it is
useless to try to describe them, struggle off her sofa
to pull down the shade that has separated us ever since,
her room as lonely as Keats' room on the Piazza di Spagna
where there was hardly any space for words, where I snapped
a forbidden photo that later showed nothing of his shadow
making its way to a window above Berninni's fountain,
a shadow that hesitated as if to open one of Fanny Brawne's
letters before deciding to take them to the grave unread,
who knew how little his own death must mean to the boys playing
in the Piazza below, a shadow that I later understood as
my own, indecipherable, but I just wanted to tell you about
that other day, the ordinary one, when the drunk turned over
under the local papers beneath a bush in the park, when another
in a T-shirt, tattooed, picked up the paper to check
the lottery number, then put it down, secure it was
just another ordinary day, that happy day in which
nothing left my shadow, that sorrowful day in which
nothing entered, while I took my mother to the clinic at noon
to burn away the spot on her lungs not nearly as large
as the one Keats fought, walked along the river alone,
bought broccoli for my favorite soup, and good wine,
hummed a pitiful song unconsciously, on that day
when a few million cells in each living thing died

and were replaced perfectly, when I wrote a few words,
crossed them out, wrote others, that day, I can tell you
now, when someone left a bunch of yellow flowers, buttercups,
on the grave of a nameless child burned forty years ago
in a circus fire, leaving also the child's name, Sarah,
which is why I remember that other day, because it seems
if her story could be known thousands of other ordinary days
that belonged to her might also be known, and I could tell
my daughter why I have this sudden desire to weep
all day, why I weep for the names of the dead continuing,
Samir Sayah, 16, shot in the stomach by soldiers,
Amyad Nafea, 18, shot in the chest by soldiers the moment
while my cat scratched the door, while the cicadas
began their afternoon thrumming on that ordinary day
where I found myself powerless and guilty once again,
a day so ordinary the descendants of the very lice that bothered
Christ began their work in the hair of the boy trying
to outrun the soldiers, an ordinary day, yes, when it was
not so impossible to go looking for the dead, though
I must say that of all the deaths that inhabit me
the one the other day was the least noticed lately,
so small that I imagined myself alive all day,
holding a yellow flower, just one, just to remember,
a day I can almost forget except for its likeness to today,
a day I must call ordinary because if it is not so
ordinary, then Christ, we are pitiful for our poor laments,
the deaths so small we must imagine ourselves alive all day.

Hope

I am going to talk about hope
—Cesar Vallejo

. . .fogged in with hope
—Paul Celan

When I give the few dinars to the little pharaohs,
if we call these two gypsies by their right name,
when the boy tries to pull his sister away so that she
stares wide eyed at me, I cannot help thinking of
those photos of the poor gypsies the Nazis hung in the hills
just east of here. I imagine a young man, maybe
the grandfather of these two who has been directing them
from a few yards away, I imagine him hiding with the Partisans
in Marjin Pass, fingering by candlelight the worn
letter from his son. He must see in the steam that rises
from the winter's thin stew, by the light of a shot up
moon, a scene where some future daughter of his son is
playing Chopin on her piano, where the boy is kicking
a soccer ball against the side of a school, anything
but this scene which includes me, far from home, dreaming
the way he must have, wondering what has become of you.

At this moment, I can say each world begins when
you begin to dream. Maybe it stops. The old pharaoh is
sitting on the 600-year-old bridge of abandoned hope
in Mostar, abandoned by the architect a few days before
he finished it, who was found weeping beside the grave
he would enter if it fell. He is sitting the way my father would,
flicking cigarettes the way he did, Chesterfields, without
moving his arm, *how did he do that*, I'd want to know,
into the Merrimack River in Lawrence, Mass. They were stars,
he'd say, or candles, dying to make the dusk a little
brighter, that we retrieve whenever we borrow
a little light against despair. Listen, I am borrowing
that light. I am watching my two pharaohs working
the street, how the boy keeps tugging at her dress to make
her look more desperate. I am looking beyond them,
towards the grave of the poet whose name I hardly pronounce,

who fought for the poor. I am lighting this candle for him.
And I am looking towards our poet, towards Cesar Vallejo—
"Down the road my heart is walking on foot,"
he wrote, the poet who never lived where he was,
who knew, years before, how he'd die in Paris in the rain.
I see him as a child no older than these pharaohs, in Santiago
de Chuco, Peru, four days by horseback to the nearest
railbed, another day to the coast. One evening, he watches
a peasant being beaten for a few pesos, for a few words,
and knows, too, the future exile who will wander inside him.

Maybe it is impossible to live in one moment at a time.
Maybe Vallejo was right, that every moment we have is
a past we make into a future, or a future we must bless.
That is why I think each dream is a hope we have
that we are not where we are. Each dream, my father
would say, is a dream of travel. Once by the Merrimack
we found the empty shells of beetles, dozens of them,
and he explained how they had been abandoned by horsehair
worms that grew three feet in their bellies, spiraling
like DNA until, almost becoming beetles themselves,
they abandoned one dream for another. To know anything,
he said, even love, is to know what lives inside it,
to know how we live inside each other, the terror
of any life. I did not understand that until this morning,
reading how Celan's poems grew smaller and smaller,
how he was afraid to talk directly because he feared
the Nazis were still listening, how his poems were codes
against despair. Certainly the pharaohs know that. I have
not forgotten these two, working their way back through
the crowd, handing the few coins to the grandfather,
handing over the years, the lives any moment holds.

I am handing this over to you, *whoever you are*, as
Whitman said, fearing *you are walking the walks of dreams*,
Handing this poem, like a dream, like a little candle for the dark.
I am imagining the little pharaoh at her piano after all,
playing Chopin as her grandfather dreamed, I am thinking
of Chopin, beginning the second piano concerto, how
the piano seems to wait, awed by the orchestra's beauty,

or how the orchestra itself holds off what it knows will be
the plaintive entrance of the piano, how each gesture includes
the other. It was Chopin, like Vallejo, who would die
in Paris, in the rain, who was buried with a fistful of Polish
dirt, to stop, he hoped, his soul from wandering.

I am handing this over to you, a story for another time.
I no longer care what tense it is, what places we are
speaking from. What is any story but a form of hope?
Think even of the story of Osip Mandelstam, exiled
twice, tortured, how he asked in his last days only for
some candles and blankets. In one version he is thrown
out of the barracks by the other prisoners when he eats
their food, fearing the guards have poisoned his. His eyes
sink even deeper into his face than those haunting photos
of his early years, than the photos of gypsies, than the eyes
of my little pharaoh. He is living near the camp refuse heap
as winter approaches, the long gray beard beginning
to stiffen with sorrow, the gypsy of Vladivostok, still
making the hopeful poems he says only to himself.
One day he will look out to see *mounds of human heads*
wandering into the distance, and then himself out there,
dwindling among them, unseen, but perhaps rising again
from the dead, from his own poems, to see the sun starting.
He is hoping to find out what it means to live. He is
dreaming of sleighs, the shy currents of boyhood streams,
knowing how the earth is always ready to take him back.

By now the little pharaohs have crossed over the bridge
of abandoned hope and have dissolved like Mandelstam into night.
They have dissolved like Vallejo who tried to love everyone,
whoever is crying for death, whoever is crying for water,
who would die, as he knew, from a pain that came from
everywhere that Good Friday, 1938, the way the world was.
I would make them appear again, maybe later, maybe Belgrade,
in the faces of the pharaohs who will run beside us, selling
flowers, jewelry, anything, in a city the Nazis tried
to steal. They will never be the pharaohs of Egypt though
they keep their secrets as closed as the hidden chambers
of pyramids. I am thinking of the small cave, the small room

outside the Church of St. Peter in Belgrade, of how I stood
beside my friend as he lit the candles for his parents, "one
for death," placing it in the sand on the floor, "but two for life,"
he says, two hanging in the urn in the middle of the air,
between earth and sky, past and future, a candle for hope.

There are no pharoahs much later where I am sitting
in the cafe in Slovenia with a poet who is telling me
over the weakening table candle in its green, gaudy cup,
how as a child he would wander the Alps, how he could
name every bird, every tree, every thing that moved,
but now his voice breaks, he lights another cigarette,
another star, and he is telling me how he watched
the Germans pull his father from the house and shoot him
there in the street, how for years he felt, as Celan did,
that he had already died, that there was no word for hope.
We could be still sitting there, trying to separate the words
we have for fear and for hope. We could still be sitting there,
trying to find the secret codes Celan used in his poems,
even the bleakest, words that meant *we are still alive.*

Look, this is a moment that is trying to speak in future
tense, the way the boats of pharaohs were meant
to carry their dreams to whatever future the god had hoped,
beyond their deaths, beyond their suffering, gathering all
time around them—as here in Mostar, Belgrade, Slovenia,—
now here in Venice where I will walk past Byron's mansion
near the old post office, where, when Teresa Guiccolli left,
he imagined her everywhere, sitting in the plush chair
in the corner, at the table with wine, along the canals.
I am standing there now. I am lighting a candle again
in the Church of St. Mark's for my little pharaohs, for Vallejo,
the gypsy poet who would walk brooding alone for hours,
for Mandelstam, who could find hope in the garbage of a prison
camp, for the sweet music of Chopin, I am lighting it
for all of us, handing it over to the memory of Celan,
and handing it over equally to the future of Celan,
to our undreamt dreams, I am lighting this candle for all,
of us, a little light against despair, a little blessing for love,
a candle for our deaths, a candle for our lives, a candle for hope.

Shadows

Why is there something rather than nothing?
            —Parmenides

What a consoling poem this will be if the roadside
crows that scatter into the pines as each car passes,
that rise like the souls of the dead in Van Gogh's wide
and confused heaven, are not the signs of your loss.
What a consoling poem this might be if I could remember
the first secret place where the pitiful world did not,
as Flaubert says it does, surface in terrible error
like the bloated bodies of dogs in a stream near his retreat
at Rouen, those poor shadows of the dead, despite
the stones tied to their necks, and surface in the sentences
Flaubert wrote trying to find a secret place for each right
word, a place that did not mean the old disgust for happiness.
I thought I had seen death. I see instead those rising crows
again, remember your leaving, and, scattered here, in shadows
that fall across this page, figures I'd forgotten, shadows
that seem to rise from the faded newsprint, that seem to show
how each private loss is part of a larger loss we might
remember. Yesterday's news is the young boy in Providence
R.I., who followed the consoling words of some killer one night
into woods where animals later tore off his face, or two Palestinians,
two boys, faces covered, who followed one street or another
with a crowd of protesters and were shot, or how, unable to let
death take him, a Bantu tribesman clutched the dirt of his father,
lifting himself again so the Pretoria soldiers could not forget.
Listen, it is nearly dawn here, and I wish the losses
I am describing were never true, that the world could confide
whatever dream you might need not to abandon your past
and a few clothes on the shore, finding no words, no place to hide.

I didn't know, when you left, about poor Flaubert never finding
the words to dominate the absurd sounds of parrots he kept
hearing, the plaintive sounds of cicadas that always haunted
him, how he would mutilate phrases, how he'd shift sentences,
how each word was, he wrote, an "endless farewell to life,"
crossing out repetitions that meant he only had one voice,

that meant, really, hearing the endless terror of his own voice.
I didn't know, then, about Van Gogh, who was finding silence
in an asylum, while Flaubert tried to write an asylum for his life,
a style to hold off death, a style that he feared, that he kept
even from his brother. I hadn't read, then, those poor sentences
to Theo, haunted by the power of color and shape, haunted
by shadows of enemies he invented, the way the birds haunt
his last painting, *Crows Over a Wheatfield*, where the lost voice
of Christ seems to dissolve into darkness that moment his sentence
was finished, those crows that could be flying towards us, finding
only our losses, or up towards heaven, or maybe they keep
wavering, flying both ways at once, the way Van Gogh's life
would, as he himself knew, painting, he wrote, his own life
in theirs. I can't help but wonder how those crows haunt
all his last paintings. I believe he must have found a way to keep
a secret place somewhere on each canvas, the way Christ's voice
seems to hide beneath the thick paint. I believe he must have found
how the birds carry the painting away from itself, as Flaubert's sentences
were meant to lead him away from what he called the sentence
of his life. And because he saw a halo shimmering around each life
or object the way he had as a young preacher, what did Van Gogh find,
what consolation against all that pain? I am still haunted
by that faceless boy in Providence, the African without a voice,
the Palestinian boys kept from their homes, these deaths that keep
announcing their obscene selves. Like Flaubert, I'm going to keep
trying to find some style, some shape for these sentences.
I believe I can hear, in Van Gogh's painting, the poor voice
of Christ which is the voice, too, of Flaubert, and these lost lives
that haunt me now. I believe that the last demon that haunted
Van Gogh was his fear that, outside his frames, nothing was found
to keep the "troubled skies" from his life, nothing even
in his sentences to Theo—"what's the use?" he asked hauntingly,
finally, like the voice of Christ, crying to be found.

Listen, I am writing to you now, on this table crossed
by shadows, that the answer is anyone hearing your voice,
anyone hoping the next news of you is not your loss,
trying by these repetitions to call you back, though the place
keeps shifting because I can't hide the world Flaubert, at Rouen,
fought inside each phrase, and you wouldn't believe a story

with no suicide or death. Here I am again
thinking of Van Gogh, listening to Lightin' Hopkins say
the blues are everywhere, the blues are us, these stories
he sings on the scratched tape, the stories we read
about Van Gogh, the headlines, the poems, the way
the blues rhythms never change, 4/4, as if we needed
something that constant against our fears, as if we knew
how much these sad stories showed us what it means
to go on. Here I am again, listening to the blues,
starting to understand it is my own despair I seem
to fight. Last night, I stood on the bridge where a friend
dove into the shadows of the Tennessee and was afraid
I could agree at last. I was thinking of the faceless boy again,
remembering how the man who found him by the pond where he lay
face down, turned him over, saw what the animals had done
and knelt in prayer, knelt for the pity of it, for the faces
of everyone dead or missing, knowing how he must go on.

I was thinking, too, how the mothers of the Palestinian boys
must also have knelt, must have touched the life
leaking from them, must also have prayed, unwrapped
the cloth around their heads hoping some other life,
not a son's, was missing. I have been thinking how the map
of this table, ever since you left, scatters the shadows
of what we must have talked about, and how Van Gogh's
pictures, the dark secret places in Flaubert's phrases, show
all our words as a care for life, a color we have to hold.

I can't forget that faceless boy. I can't stop wondering
what last thing he touched or saw. I get up, punch
another tape into the player, Charlie Parker, "the Bird,"
taking off into rhythms and harmonies more unpredictable
than Van Gogh's crows—taking notes from what he touched or saw—
dogs barking, the hiss of a radiator, the sudden squeal
of a train's brakes, the rhythm and harmonies of the unpredictable
drunk shifting in a doorway, changing every sad thing
so that the dog's barking, the hiss of the radiator, the squeal
of brakes becomes not a sign of loneliness or loss, but joy,
the notes shifting like Flaubert's words, like the drunk in the doorway,
discovering in each phrase and note some secret place

among the flattened fifths meaning either loss or joy,
among the odd intervals of chords his alto sax remembers,
until he fell asleep for good in an armchair in New York,
nearly 35, "I'm just a husk," he said, in the end, just a phrase
or note you remember, and I do, in this poem for you,
taking these hints from the flights of the bird, Charlie Parker,
who lived beyond his own death in each note, flying on those notes
above the deaths of the boy, the Palestinians, the tribesmen.

I remember last summer, finding an old sax player
just waking among the remnants of fieldstone cellars
some quarry workers left half a century ago outside
Gloucester, Mass., a place called *Dogtown*, where he tried
among the sounds of stray dogs Parker would have loved,
to remember the clear notes of the alto sax rising above
the trees, above his memory of the war, unable to sleep
without checking the perimeter, each hour, to keep
all the shadows named and held, unable to sleep at all
if it rained because he couldn't hear the enemy's footfall.
And I am remembering the Bantu tribesman, how he could
tell immediately that the difference between dirt and blood
no longer mattered, that the lost children he fought for,
the child detained for questioning and found weeks later
among the smoldering garbage, his tongue cut out
for talking to newsmen, were what his death might be about,
a death that gathered above the tin roofs as the past gathered
—maybe the way it gathered in the eyes of the sax player
who could not forget, as he told it, the way his base
camp was overrun, the way, after a while, the haze
he was seeing was not dawn, not even the smoke of rifles,
but the unbelievable smoke of bodies burning, and the terrible
vapor that rose from open wounds, the sickening stink
that took the place of words, screams, whatever you tried to think.
When things were bad, he said, he could remember the service
for William Williams in New Orleans, how the entire brass
had gathered for the long march to Carrollton cemetery—
the Eureka Brass Band—with its slow dirges, its heavy
hymn notes to "In the Sweet Bye and Bye," the trombones
leading the way, he and his father among the baritone
horns of the second rank—and how they danced on the way

home to "St. Louis Blues," music, he said, you could raise
the dead with, as now, he just wanted once more to hear
the consoling notes of Parker, some sound to drive away his fear.

Listen, I have tried to find for us a shape for all this grief,
a form to make, as Parker and Van Gogh did, our fear
into a strength. It may be that any form is a kind of belief
that the losses, the shadows on this table, the enemy we fear
when the world goes dark, can be contained beyond our moment.
In Berea, Ohio, once, I came across an old graveyard
next to a quarry, centered by a concubine pine, a tree
that grew around its own cones and branches that were bent
around the trunk, as if the tree took as its form the discarded
parts of its own past and future, while all around the tree
the failed graveyard gave a few coffins, whenever it rained,
to the quarry, though now its whole past has been retrieved.
Today, I want to tell you about the sax player's sad grin,
I want to kneel with him before all these shadows that will flee
if only we can name them, to tell you about another friend, torn coat,
hovering in a doorstep in Belgrade before he escaped the Russians,
how he'd twist gunpowder out of shells to sell to gangs for bread,
how he watched a kneeling soldier smile to slit a prisoner's throat,
how he chose not the Danube, but life. Not long ago I knelt in
the park where he played, one secret place where finally the dead
were only distant shadows. I was feeding the few ragged crows
that could have been Van Gogh's birds, leaving them a little bread
and cheese, thinking again of you, of your sadness, of how
form may be only, as Whitman said, another name for the body,
for all the secret places we contain, the only consolation we have known,—
and I was gathering you around me, building my own secret place
inside you, feeling you move again unpredictably, like Parker's
rhythms, the shifts in Flaubert's sentences, knowing, having known,
that this poem begins in our fear and ends in the same place,
feeling the world move, trying to stay this way forever.

For a Long Time I Have Wanted
to Write a Happy Poem

Between two worlds life hovers like a star.
—Byron

It is not so easy to live on the earth
as an angel, to imitate the insects that dance
around the moon, to return what air we borrow
every few seconds. I am going to enter
the hour when wind dreamt of a light dress
to stroke, when water dreamt of the lips it would meet.
The famous Pascalian worm will just have to find
another heart to eat.
I will reveal the actual reason birds fly off
so suddenly from telephone wires.
The road will ask my foot for help.
The lightning will forget its thunder.
I will discover the hidden planet
to account for Pluto's eccentric orbit.
Pluto, of course, is ready to leave the alliance.
I learned this from a recent *Scientific American*.
No longer will I have to lament
the death of Mary, the circus elephant,
hung with chains from a derrick on Sept. 16, 1916,
in Erwin, Tennessee to punish her immortal soul
for brushing her keeper to death.
She looks out from her daguerreotype
as if she knows one day we too will hear
the stars gnaw away at our darkness.
It is not so easy.
One day I will free the clouds frozen in ponds.
No longer will the wind lose its way.
I will start hearing important voices like a real saint.
The king of Kuwait will answer my call.
If I am not careful I will loosen
the noose of history from around my own neck.
Just to keep sane I will have to include my weight
which is the only thing that keeps me from being a bird.

Walking on air will no longer be a problem.
Meanwhile, the Hubble telescope is still wobbling
its pictures from outer space so we will
have to rely on imagination a little longer to see clearly.
Why don't windows tell us everything they see?
Here come the characters of my sad poems.
They have been standing in line to get in
like fans for a rock concert.
They are gathering around Beatrix Potter who spent 30 years
locked in her room. The maid brings up her supper.
She sneaks out into the garden to capture
small animals to draw or reinvent before they die.
Beatrix, I say, we no longer have to kill what we see.
I know this in my heart, in my wolf, in my owl.
In the Siena of my palms. The Bergamo of my head.
In the garlic of my fingers. My friends say
I use too much. There are never enough
streets crossing the one we are stuck on.
No one wants to be a cloud anymore.
Who still believes in the transmigration of souls?
If you believe Bell's theorem, then the fact is
that the squirrel falling out of my tree this morning
makes minute sub-atomic changes from here to Australia.
Will I have to put on my pants differently now?
Just when we start to believe in moonlight
we notice how many stars it erases. It is not easy.
I am going to come back
as the birthmark on the inside of your thigh,
between your dreams of angels and solar dust,
between your drunken skirt and the one that laughs.
I am going to learn what the butterfly knows
about disguise, what so astonishes the hills.
All this is going to take constant vigilance.
In "The Last Chance Saloon," Tombstone, Arizona,
I saw the lizard creature with its glued head,
almost human, tilted up from under the glass,
as if it didn't know which world to claim.
Apparently it fooled a lot of people in 1872.
I kept thinking if only Ovid had seen this creature
he would have known his nymphs

could never escape just by turning into trees.
In Dora Noar, Afghanistan, the young soldier,
Mohammad Anwar, age 13, believes he will turn
into a desert flower when he dies in the jihad.
The barrel of his AK-47 is sawed down
because he is as small as the four prisoners
he has returned with. They understand
that all we know of the sky we learn by listening to roots.
"I was happy," he says after shooting them
against a wall, over and over again, "I was happy."
Happy. Now maybe the Earth will want to change its name.
It won't want to be the Earth anymore.
Shadows will be abandoned by their objects.
The light will squander itself on the flowers
because they do not even want to be flowers anymore.
It is not easy to live on this earth.
We don't understand that the universe is
blowing away from us like litter,
but at an incredible speed.
There is a new theory that the universe is left-handed.
It has to do with the spin of quarks.
Someone else says it's in the form of a horseshoe.
The rest of the animal is metamorphosed into a black hole.
I happen to side with the fanatics who believe
it is following the call of a mythic bird too distant to see,
but this is only poetry, like the old papers
the homeless use to stuff their clothes on cold nights,
the kind of poetry that says, flowers, be happy,
trees, raise your drooping eyebrows,
sky, don't turn your back on us again,
my love, how wonderful to have lived while you lived,
which is not the sort of poetry you read anyplace anymore.

WORLDS APART

(1987)

Unable to Refuse

Some places we can't refuse. This is the night
I never arrived, never called, and even a few hours after
the storm the trees are trying to tell me things
I don't want to hear. The land around is empty with
sinkholes, what a chart on the wall says are
the slow crumbling of the limestone base. This is the place
where the earth sucks in fences, rusted hay rakers,
barns leaning on braces of 4 x 8's for a few years
to delay but not refuse geography. It's the farmers
who make best use of them—filling the holes with
garbage, cuttings, even old cars that disappear
after several months or years. Here the dirty earth
pulls in everything, covers it over, turns it into
itself, so you don't refuse anything, not even love.

At least that's what the woman at the end of the counter
tries to tell everyone here as long as the storm has kept us
together, and maybe she's right. At least it's a word
that gets taken in by others—the way it is spoken in
anything *sloven*, like the young drunk knocking hell
out of the condom machine in the trucker's restroom
planning to climb into some girl as if she were earth,
or even the beautiful *plover* that's just threatening to re-emerge.

The newspaper the woman holds announces the death of the young
boy who re-emerged from his bubble chamber south of here:
"Bubble Boy Loses Battle in Dirty World," and really,
the world is dirty, at least here where the boy has never
been to refuse any earth, who has barely walked
on grass, never mind this sinking land.

                  So this is the place
I've come to, trapped inside a truck stop until the earth
refuses or accepts me, keeping me from home, listening
to things I don't want to hear—the woman at the counter
talking about the boy and love in the same breath,
yet thinking how wrong it is to refuse anything after all,
and how, those times we refused each other, we seemed to disappear.

Worlds Apart

I can't help but believe the killdeer,
so deftly has it led me,
dragging its own wings away from a poorly
hidden nest before clenching back into flight,
and I can't help but believe in a love
that would make itself so vulnerable for its young.

It is hard to understand, but
only by leaving do we know what we love.

Before I left, you told the story
of the fledgling cuckoo who hatches on a sparrow's
nest, who spills out the native fledglings,
and is adopted by the vulnerable parents.
One night, in a city far from home,
I watched in amazement as two young men
who seemed more fierce than the cuckoo,
stooped to kiss some bag lady on the forehead
and pass her a dollar, a lady who had nested on a corner
with her dozen sacks and a cart.

Never have I felt so guilty
for what little love I could show.
That night, alone on a bus, I thought
you were the starlight nesting in the trees
holding every moment of your life.

In the pine woods along the coast north of here
starlight never touches the ground.
Somewhere in there the cuckoo will begin to sing.
I don't think there was ever a time we weren't
approaching each other through those woods.
I don't think there is a moment we have
that is not taking place somewhere else,
or a love that doesn't lead us, sometimes
deftly, further from ourselves.

The Promise of Light

In the background, steam rises from the snow patches,
and from the backs of horses nearly out of sight
yet making their way towards a hidden stream.
For a moment, the crowd that is gathered around the man
who drank himself to death does not know whether
to look at this and the other pictures he painted
at the end of this alley in perfect detail, or at the man.

I believe the artist painted his scenes from Gustav Mahler's
Pastoral, and it must be that by now the horses
would have found the stream, so much do they seem to trust
the artist's stroke which allows them all to turn
away, perhaps from shyness. Once, north of Atlanta,
I came upon two trailers in a wreck that had spilled
their horses, quiet and unnatural, on the wet pavement,

lit at intervals by the blue lights of the police cruisers.
No doubt these horses waiting to disappear into
the wall are those horses alive in a world we can't name,
and this man, who kept a photograph of a woman he never
knew, cut from a magazine, as his friends explain,
speaking his whole life to her, invented whatever
past, whatever future, he could trust to face the dark.

And surely he remembered, for the first time in years,
climbing the ladder down to the bottom of a pier—
the stars already fading—with a girl he hardly
knew, the wooden pilings coated with barnacles
and black seaweed, the tide low, the oil slicks
gathering on the harbor around driftwood, paper
cups, tin cans, dead fish—gathering towards

the darkness which was the other shore they swam for,
trusting luck, trusting the certainty of tides. He must
have remembered how long it takes to trust anything.

I remember reading how Mahler as a boy watched until dawn,
not believing in the burlap bags stuffed with the hair
of mice and human hair—charms his uncle hung
around the orchard because nuisance deer couldn't stand the smell.

Now, in silence, the crowd begins to break up. The artist
who had seemed only to be sitting asleep on a cinder
block he took from an empty lot next door is gone,
and I almost believe the fog on the walls might lift,
revealing the scene I read once where Mahler watched,
from a distance, a girl so awkwardly beautiful he couldn't
trust what he saw. The man with her lifted her blouse

and placed it across a branch, its arms spread
like antlers, or spread like the arms of another lover,
or her father, or even Mahler becoming too slowly the man
who would finally understand that whoever you love is
all of a sudden there, promising nothing but the next day,
the way fireflies would gather as they all began
to leave, promising nothing but their own brief light.

In those days, the imprints from tie beams in the shadow
of a railbed in Bohemia would be enough to take him anywhere.
Once, by tracks like those, I found and broke open a brown cocoon—
inside were hundreds of yellow spiders entangled in each
other's lives, the way our own lives and the lives
of so many we never knew, even this poor artist's,
become entangled by whatever stories we remember.

I remember the story of Gustav Mahler writing
his pastoral symphony in a world as silent as this wall,
instructing his wife to untie the bells from cows,
cut the rope to the village tower, teach singers
how to mime—and how she would try to silence the birds, keep
the horses from running—and how, later, he would lock himself
in a room waiting for his daughter to die, and how he would return

to the Danube to face his own lingering death. And I remember
Mike Connally, the sketch artist who played left field
with an old, stubby glove and whom we called "Sky" because of the long

fly balls he'd hit, and how he turned away, in the end, from
any sky to face the quiet of the Tennessee for three weeks before
they found him. I think he knew what the poet Delmore Schwartz meant
by the deafness of solitude, the world we are never able to hear—

Schwartz, who wrote on a restroom wall in Syracuse, New York,
"Give me $5 and the change and I'll go where the morning
and the evening can't hurt me," and who lay finally
for three days in a New York City morgue. We live
so seldom in the real world, he said, because we are
so often surprised by the deaths of friends, and cannot
understand, even from that, the meaning of our own deaths.

It may be that now I no longer wish to tell one event
from another, believing the stars which are moving away
yet reappear, like the stories of this artist, of Mahler, of Schwartz,
and of Mike Connally. On the far wall is a picture of wolves
who must have stalked a caribou to death for weeks,
trusting, even as the artist must have, in the terrible
meaning of that event, trusting, as we must, in the way

the mind and heart find each other out
despite our own fears, despite whatever details
we invent to divert ourselves, these stories or images
we make of the morning emerging from the fog where,
when we look carefully, one or the other of us is
also emerging, trusting whatever silence lingers,
knowing the world begins from where we are.

Raspberries

The old man knows the earth is not a dream.
He is not going to read my poem about the tiny
brown and yellow saw-whet owl, silent,
as it often is by day behind the flute sounds
of my daughter's practice, nor will he listen to any
self-indulgence about whether it cares if I'm here.

Instead, he is stockpiling old painkillers
to prescribe the time of his own death. This morning,
the old man showed me his palms stained like a map
by raspberries he was selling, and I remembered how
I used to believe that the souls of suicides wandered
a geography not even Parmenides could name.
He wasn't going to say what he believed. He wasn't
going to tell his wife when the pain became too great.
Behind him, the cracks in the window frames of his shack
were stuffed with wads of paper to keep the hornets
and wasps from going after the berries, and I could see,
still, my own father, how he'd protect the preserves
in our cellar—peach, strawberry, grape, raspberry,
blueberry, holding the whole summer by stockpiling
the sunlight, he'd say, for the winter's dark cold,
the winter's silence.
                    But this old man, he wasn't
going to hold on to the past, he only wanted to talk about
how the earth had fallen apart along that coast, the glaciers
rotted from the insides, trailing the long gravel beds
down the sides of hills, how the walls of those cliffs
tell us the life we have is only a few centimeters in rock.

He wasn't going to read my poem, but I have left him in
here, sitting with a few wooden boxes at his roadside
stand. And why not? I don't know any longer what will be
important—tonight my daughter rushed in here
from practicing with news her friend's heart had suddenly
failed. I wanted the stain of a father's love to hold
longer than I knew it would. What could I tell her?
A few years ago, when legend, not geography, held us,
I would tell her the Indian stories for death—
how the father of Shining Waters was the Sun,
how her young lover saved her father's home
dispelling the birds of darkness by his own death.
I had forgotten until now how we have to invent
a life for the dead.
      I had doubted, when I began,
that Parmenides was right to say that what we thought
became the world we lived, but when you look
carefully, markings set by men or time in rocks,
objects in legends or poems, tell you whatever story
you want them to. This morning I believed it was
only a question of not using such a tired symbol
of loneliness and despair as that owl. Now,
as my daughter reads the notes they passed
in school, their children's jokes, the message to remember
Jennifer whenever she played, she is trying to find
the words to hold her close.
      Do you know what I'm saying?
I am trying to find for her what secret words
preserve our pasts, what secret brings the owl back
again to these lines where it doesn't seem to belong.
I had seen it before. Years ago, the woman across
the unpaved street that would be covered late that summer,
the same woman who was beating an old Persian rug
she'd strung across the cast iron bars of the clothesline,
looked up and saw the small owl that must have tangled
itself in the rope lines. She looked up and knew the cancer
deep in her liver, knew, I believe, it would take her in a week.
In those days, when we ate bread soaked in milk,
when we bottled root beer in sarsaparilla bottles and waited
for the street to be paved or tarred, while the neighborhood

grew and the owls disappeared, I held my mother, afraid
that she, too, might die. It was the summer we walked
along the railroad tracks picking raspberries for miles
of happiness, hearing my father scratch a song on the harmonica
trying to make us forget the woman whose name is lost now,
and the boy who would ride his bike beneath the tar truck,
his face burned to a mask, and the neighbor who parachuted
into the Korean sea, all the faces that return now faster
than I want them to.
                  So this is it, this is why I am
going to include all this in that old poem for another summer,
as Parmenides would, why I am going to let the owl,
then or now, speak for whatever future rises from the trees,
itself rising, as Parmenides does in the fragments of his own
lost poem, to escape the geography of grief, the dark
that gathers, anyways, failing what we hoped for it,
why I am going to tell the old man how any breath,
however pained, is what Jennifer would choose, why I am
going to listen to the sound of my daughter's flute
rising like the old legends, setting like a stain in the air,
as the owl lifts a wing, as we all move off, becoming
a few lines in the rock, holding whatever stories
keep us safe, into the silent worlds we hold so dear.

Today a Few Years from Now

There will always be the same man we saw selling winter
coats to the Salvation Army and buying back bright summer
jackets, mismatched, yellowed at the edges, smelling
of mothballs, smelling of new hope, the nights not spent
sleeping over the grates of the Lovemans' store exhaust.
There will always be the talk about poems, this morning
about Edmund Blunden, all his green details trying
to cover over the trenches of his past—ours and death's,
he called them—the gassed bodies stuck in poses that asked
questions too bizarre to answer, the bloated mules lining
the paths where the supply trains were shelled. I don't see
how he kept, as he said he would, the mind from drooping.
I am looking now at the flyer that has come in the bulk mail
to announce the "Revelation Lectures," Biblical prophecy,
a vision of terror that Blunden so feared. I am looking
at the white moon against the blue sky and I remember
how long it has been since I noticed that. There will always be
that moon, Blunden's green poems, the way you keep close
the flat truth of our shadows which is also Blunden's way to find
in any darkness, a self to forgive. There will always be this
stupid horned lark caught, as I write to you, on the porch,
flying against the screen like a moth, its mate flying against
the other side, until I poke a hole in the screen for its escape.
In the background it is Robert Schumann, a cello concerto,
Schumann, who wrote so joyfully to escape the bleak
and failing porch of his own mind, who practiced for hours
tying one finger in a sling to improve his reach, but who
crippled all hopes of playing his own music, who tried to find
places where there was so little to hear he might desire
again to write. For him, the past could be the silence we feel
with whatever songs, whatever memories we hold or invent.
That is why I must tell you that this moment goes back
to where I found as a boy a lark caught in the rusted
springs of an abandoned Buick, remembered, even then,
the earlier car on my way home from little league

practice, the whole car rocking with the two inside it
as if something invisible drove it along the road to the park.
There will always be that boy's wonder to feel what it meant
for the girl to cry, as surely as that lark, afterwards.
I wanted to climb into the backseat, to hold the girl beneath me,
the car moving towards whatever worlds I could dream.
There will always be a moment like that arriving, some face
that means the shining love of loss, that means the first awkward
shifting of lovers, and the wonder, as if it were from a life
someone else had lived, as if, in the face of some fear or hope
we could split apart as Plato says we did once before,
or become like the sea cucumber you described once:
facing a mortal danger it splits itself in two, one half to die,
one half to live. I think this is what poor Blunden meant by the second
night
behind the first. I think this is what Schumann knew
when he became the several characters he hid behind to write,
when he believed the great composers dictated his music.
I think this is what my father meant when he confessed
another life, years earlier, to explain the Buick. I hardly
understood, could only watch his embarrassed face across
the fire, his trying to say a few words disguised as talk
about the night, about the liver and the few fish jumping,
the names of stars, baseball, things that meant, finally,
that you don't hurt anyone, you don't forget the girl in the Buick,
the man sleeping across the grates, whomever you hurt
by intention or neglect. I am remembering all this today.
I am holding the newspaper telling the death of Norm Cash,
my father's hero, who led the league at .361. I am wishing
I could share that loss with him, or at least lean over some
wilderness fire to say how much of his life is hidden
in my own. There will always be this Schumann playing,
and for a few minutes I can imagine myself as he did,
fearing there would be no more songs, or only our lark's
muted song, so he walks into the Rhine, is pulled out later
by fishermen before committing himself to the asylum
at Edenrich. There was the smell of fish, the slick banks
of the river, the blankets they threw across him like netting.
And there would be for him two more years trying to figure out
the coded messages he had once spelled out in his musical

notes, the way we try to find one thing in another, what
the bird on the porch or the bird in the Buick will tell us,
the way Blunden tried to escape the terror of his own past,
discovering, finally, that every life is our own life, the way
the faint whistle of the lark becomes part of Schumann's
concerto, the song which means nothing or means everything
it touches, as Schumann must have figured out that last day,
the porcelain bowl beside his table reflecting what little
light was left, the blue flowers on its sides reminding him
of distant fields, of the way his wife played the songs he couldn't,
unable to find anything that day might mean in the years ahead,
a day as ordinary as this, filled with failed hopes and songs,
a day ending while the notes meant only themselves, July 29, 1859.

What to Listen For

Who listens when we talk? This is a question
Pascal asked, and answered only with the safe
bet that someone must, and the question I asked
when I went through the rain this morning to study
the museum photographs of Nazca ground drawings
taken from a plane over Peru. Etched from the dry
pampa, these enormous caterpillars, whales, foxes,
turtles, and the animals and insects no one has seen
before, were meant to evoke some response from the gods.
Which explains why they have been so carefully revised.
Which explains, too, why they were never finished.
It is still raining. How long has he been singing,
that yellow-billed cuckoo, while I have been thinking,
again, of what you said. The farmers call it a *rain crow*
because it signals approaching storms, and because
it continues, as now, arguing against the way
the rain strips the October trees. It must be calling
from the abandoned orchard, its rapid song slowing
down at the end of each burst, as if to say how it
understands the way any love is also the beginning of loss.
Once as a boy I listened as my father explained
that the snapping turtle covered with leeches we saw
slip off the bank hadn't long to live. I hardly
heard him, could only imagine the pain I thought
it felt trying to evade the slow passage
of one life into another, and felt, too, my own
life pass over into the pond. I hardly heard him.
But I think he knew, talking only to let me know
he was there. I don't think the rain crow will stop.
I think he wants to say how easy all this is,
and not enough. Today I thought you almost wept
to describe the way it seems we had drifted apart.
Nothing is ever finished. Let's take Pascal's
faith that someone is always listening, let's know
distance as something we begin to understand each time

we extend an arm in love or consolation. I could be
saying anything to you now, because I only want
to let you know I am here, that I am arguing
against the beginning of loss, against whatever silence
threatens us, using the song of this elusive bird
to say what it would mean if you went away.

PART OF THE STORY

(1983)

The Pike and the Pickerel

For Robert Pack

He was speaking of the pike and the pickerel
that dart beneath the surface of the water
and he can almost hear the words now
as if they clung to the trees and the moss,
always on one side, meaning nothing
that words mean but knowing the way,

and he listens now as his own words move away
from him as the pike moves, as the pickerel,
as the pickerel and the pike reveal nothing
of the ways in which they color the water
with the glitter of their turning, reflecting now
the red of the leaves, now the green of the moss.

It is October. A whiteness has spotted the moss
and leaves though their color stays. It is this way
every October, and it is this way now
for him, for his words: pike and pickerel.
Therefore, though his words cross the lake meaning nothing
they are white red, white green on the water.

It is October. The wind has spotted the water
white as the spots on the leaves and moss.
His words repeat themselves as if nothing
had changed, but beneath them, the way
the whiteness has changed the leaves and moss now,
his words become those of the pike and the pickerel.

And beneath the lake the pike and the pickerel
turn in the hidden currents of the water
as if they themselves were water, and now,
they alter the reflections of the leaves and moss
as they move fluently, meaning nothing
that words could mean, but knowing their way.

And he is listening to the way
his words have become the pike and pickerel
though the pickerel and pike mean nothing
except as they turn and glitter in the water,
and he is listening to the way his words change now
as the fish change and are changed by the leaves and moss.

Across the water there is no sound, nothing.
But the words are in the leaves, the moss, in him now,
in the silent way of the pike and the pickerel.

ABOUT THE AUTHOR

Richard Jackson is the author of fifteen books of poetry including *Where the Wind Comes From* (Kelsay Books, 2021) and *Broken Horizons* (Press 53, 2018) and twelve books of essays, interviews, translations and anthologies. Other books include: *Take Five* (Finishing Line, with four other poets, 2019), *Traversings* (Anchor and Plume, 2016) *Retrievals* (C&R Press, 2014), *Out of Place* (Ashland, 2014), *Resonancia* (Barcelona, 2014, a translation of *Resonance* from Ashland, 2010), *Half Lives: Petrarchan Poems* (Autumn House, 2004), *Unauthorized Autobiography: New and Selected Poems* (Ashland, 2003), and *Heartwall* (UMass, Juniper Prize 2000), as well as four chapbook adaptations from Pavese and other Italian poets, and a chapbook of prose poems, *Fifties. The Heart's Many* Doors is an anthology of poems by American poets on the artists Metka Krašovec *(Wings Press, 2017).* He has translated a book of poems by Alexsander Persolja (*Potvanje Sonca / Journey of the Sun*) (Kulturno Drustvo Vilenica: Slovenia, 2007) as well as *Last Voyage*, a book of translations of the early-twentieth-century Italian poet, Giovanni Pascoli, (Red Hen, 2010). In addition, he has edited the selected poems of Slovene poet, Iztok Osijnik.

He was awarded the Order of Freedom Medal for literary and humanitarian work during the Balkan wars by the President of Slovenia during his work with the Slovene-based Peace and Sarajevo Committees of PEN International. He has received Guggenheim, Fulbright, NEA, NEH, and two Witter-Bynner fellowships, a *Prairie Schooner* Reader's Choice Award, the *Crazyhorse* Prize in Poetry; he is the winner of five Pushcart Prizes and has appeared in *Best American Poems* as well as many other anthologies.

His poems have been translated into nineteen languages including books in Slovenia and Barcelona. His books and chapbooks have won numerous awards including the Juniper Prize, Maxine Kumin Award, Cleveland State Poetry Prize, Choice Award, Agee Award and others. He has given hundreds of readings and lectures in the United States and abroad, from Hong Kong to India to Israel and eastern Europe. He has taught at the Iowa Summer Festival, The Prague Summer Workshops, and regularly at UT-Chattanooga (since 1976), where he directs the Meacham Writers' Conference. He has taught at Vermont College of Fine Arts since 1987, winning teaching awards at both schools. In 2009 he won the AWP George Garret Award for teaching and writing.

He also edited over twenty chapbooks of poems from Eastern Europe. His own poems have been translated into seventeen languages including *Worlds Apart: Selected Poems in Slovene*. He has edited three anthologies of Slovene poetry and *Poetry Miscellany*, a journal. He is the author of *Dismantling Time in Contemporary American Poetry* (Agee Prize), and *Acts of Mind: Interviews with Contemporary American Poets* (Choice Award). Originator of Vermont College of Fine Arts's Slovenia Program, he was a Fulbright Exchange poet to former Yugoslavia and returns to Europe each year with groups of students.

Thanks to Terri who is my best reader, wife and friend, and to Laura Graves, Michael Beard, Seth Courtad and Hannah Ritter for help in preparing this, to my students at the University of Tennessee at Chattanooga for years of engaging conversation and new ideas, and the students and faculty at Vermont College of Fine Arts and who continue to inspire me. Also thanks for the support of the University of Tennessee at Chattanooga for its generous support over the years.

CPSIA information can be obtained
at www.ICGtesting.com
Printed in the USA
BVHW030538220322
631814BV00002B/8

9 781950 413485